W9-DAV-719

Pulau Ubin
Ours to Treasure

First published December 2000
by SIMPLY GREEN
Blk 1B #09-15 Gillman Heights Condominium
Alexandra Road, Singapore 101001
Tel/Fax: (65) 878 0271
Email: sgreen@asia.com

© 2000 Simply Green
Reprinted May 2001

Project Director: K E Tan
Editor: Colin Cheong
Designer: Felicia Wong

Produced and designed by
EDITIONS KETANO
204 Loyang Avenue
#02-07 Singapore 509060
Email: ketano@pacific.net.sg

Colour separation by United Graphic Pte Ltd
Printed by Tien Wah Press (Pte) Limited

*All rights reserved. No part of this publication may be reproduced
or transmitted in any form or by any means, electronic or mechanical,
including photocopying, recording or any information storage and retrieval
system, without prior permission in writing from the publisher.*

ISBN: 981 04 3088 4

Endpapers: The forest canopy. Less accessible the secondary forest is located
on the western part of the island and supports a diverse wildlife.
Page 1: Red Junglefowl (*Gallus gallus*). Well-adapted to the plantations,
mangrove swamps and secondary forests, this fowl can fly and roost in trees.
Pages 2-3: Great Crested Terns (*Sterna bergii*) resting on *kelong* poles.
Pages 4-5: A beautiful sunrise silhouettes a *kelong* viewed from the
Civil Service Club chalets.

Pulau Ubin
Ours to Treasure

Chua Ee Kiam

Simply Green

To Amy, Jeremy and Jessica —
may their love for nature keep growing

Contents

FOREWORD

Conventional wisdom would suggest that nature's treasures cannot be found in densely populated urbanised areas. It would therefore surprise many people, foreign and local, to discover that Singapore is still endowed with such rich flora and fauna.

Consider the many species of butterflies that make their home at Kent Ridge Park or the coral reefs of the southern islands that survive in the waters surrounding the busiest port in the world. Consider also the birds that still find Singapore's mangroves a viable stopover for their long migratory flights.

Admittedly, these "green" pockets are far too small in size and too few in number. This makes the treasures they hold even more precious. Pulau Ubin is the last stronghold of local heritage — natural and man-made. Chua Ee Kiam's lovely book shares with us the natural wonders of Pulau Ubin and the fast-disappearing lifestyle of a bygone era. It would be a pity if this book becomes a mere record of a lost fortune and not a guide to a living legacy. Let us be inspired by this book to conserve the nature of Pulau Ubin.

Professor Tommy Koh

Opposite: On a slow boat to deeper waters and more fish, the lack of motorised power is not a problem — pure physical exertion will do. Sustainable fishing is one way to prevent depleting fish stocks.

PREFACE

My "baptism" at Pulau Ubin was a nature outing organised by the Malayan Nature Society (now Nature Society of Singapore) more than 10 years ago. I was introduced to a sparsely populated island bequeathed with extensive mangroves, secondary forests, luxuriant undergrowth and plantations of rubber and coconut. It was a haven for wildlife.

The birds, although more often heard than seen, were the highlight of that trip. With colours so vivid and so diverse, each sighting left me eager for more. It is not wise to leave your viewing scopes behind when visiting the island.

Pulau Ubin was also a menagerie. Many of the mammals and birds found in Ubin were on display in cages at the headman's house. There were civet cats, flying foxes, doves, junglefowl, wild ducks and bulbuls — creatures I had not expected to find in Singapore. But like bird parks and zoos the world over, it left me with an indelible impression — for many people, the only way to appreciate nature is to imprison nature.

I went back to the island often as my early excitement grew into an obsession. The picturesque quarry lakes with their jade-coloured waters and ochre rock walls are classic images for painting. The habitats — secondary forest and mangrove forest, a mixture of grassland and abandoned plantations — support a diverse range of wildlife. Getting to know the people of Ubin and sharing their memories has made Ubin an even more precious part of my life.

This book was seven years in the making. There have been many changes on Ubin, especially in the last two years. Some of the people may not live there anymore. Some sites are no longer accessible to the public for safety reasons.

Above: The White-bellied Fish-eagles (*Haliaeetus leucogaster*) take turns to hunt for their meals, often returning with eels, snakes or fish to feed their ravenous chicks. Nests are usually built on tall, dead trees and are often reused.

Opposite: With rapid development, sunrise may someday reveal concrete buildings instead of *kelong*, a form of sustainable fishing.

This makes every visit and every encounter unique and special. Every new sighting of some shy species reinforces the belief that there is more than meets the eye. Pulau Ubin, with its pervading sense of rural charm, deserves more than just a visit. Go, look carefully, listen — and you will find more than what this book can offer. And do it soon, before the old Ubin is gone.

Housing needs may spill over to Pulau Ubin in the future. My only wish is that this be deferred for as long as possible and until all other options are explored. For once the island is developed, it is difficult to imagine how much can be saved when so much would have been lost.

Dr Chua Ee Kiam

Opposite, left: National Police Cadets in training. Pulau Ubin is the place for outdoor adventures.

Opposite, right: A pond of water lilies make a picture of quiet calm.

Above: The Common Flameback (*Dinopium javanense*) flies from tree to tree looking for insects. Its colours are amazing — red crown, golden yellow upper-parts, streaked black and white head and body.

Left: Fishing can be full of surprises. The waters of the mangrove forest offer sanctuary to growing fishes which are often more easily caught with live bait. Sea bass are abundant and provide an unforgettable reeling experience.

Below: A reminder of nature's awesome power — a streak of lightning illuminates Pulau Ubin jetty.

11

Welcome to Ubin

Granite rocks around the jetty stand like sentinels at the main entry point to Pulau Ubin. Dawn lights up the stillness as the island awakens to the roar of boat engines, signalling the first waves of visitors that descend on the island every weekend.

It takes about ten minutes — of loud engine noise, the smell of diesel fumes and salt spray on your face — to get from the jetty at Changi Point to Pulau Ubin. While the shaky old jetties have been rebuilt in concrete over the years, the wooden bum-boats are still the same weathered craft with old car tyres hanging over the sides to cushion bumps. A boat moves out only when there are a dozen people to make the trip worth it for the boatman, unless you charter the whole vessel.

The boats rock in the green sea as passengers step off the vessels onto the Ubin jetty, some hesitating at the gap between the moving deck and the concrete jetty. Before this jetty was built, one had to walk across the sand or mudflats from boat to land. It is easy to spot the islanders, weighed down with supplies, but still stepping surely. The campers have their backpacks, the anglers their poles, the cyclists their ultra-modern mountain bikes that seem a little out of place on Ubin.

To the visitor who is cushioned by the comforts of modern living, the island seems to be in a different era. This was what Singapore was like, prior to development and industrialisation. Unlike the manicured gardens in urban Singapore, natural areas in Ubin are a little wild, relatively undisturbed and support a large variety of indigenous flora and fauna. Pulau Ubin is a feast for the senses.

Opposite: Motorised boats ply the waters between the mainland (at Changi Jetty) and Ubin. The boats will move only when filled with 12 or unless one charters the whole boat. Commuters have to brave the roar and vibration of boat engines, whiffs of diesel smoke and the occasional spray of salt water during the 10-minute ride.

Above: Visitors study a map on Ubin. Only those with a sense of adventure will learn what Ubin can offer.

Above: Four persons on a motorbike? It can only happen on Ubin, where even crash helmets are not worn. It's a convenient way for a family to go out. Many small trails are very difficult to drive through.

Right: Ubin Village offers residents and visitors amenities such as provision stores, restaurants, bicycle rental kiosks and a community centre. The National Parks Board (NParks) Information Kiosk and the Police Post are also located here. For many villagers, life revolves around the tiny village. During weekends and public holidays, this main road through the village is packed with visitors.

Opposite: Fresh coconuts can be hard to resist; plucking them yourself can be a bit of a challenge.

Explorations

Visitors are immediately drawn to the traditional wooden Chinese homes at Ubin Village. These and the Malay *kampung* remind me of my first home and childhood in Malaysia in the 1950s.

Down the road from the jetty through the heart of "town" are neat rows of mountain bikes gleaming in the morning sun. Here too are coffee shops, tackle shops and a restaurant. During weekends, this sleepy hollow suddenly springs to life.

Whilst most of my memories are of the flora and fauna, interacting with the residents in Chinese dialects and "bazaar" Malay was also memorable. Many of the residents I met were spontaneous in their hospitality and usually made time to chat, occasionally offering durians. For me, their simple living seemed a forgotten art.

Once out of Ubin Village, exposed legs and arms are vulnerable to mosquitoes. Once, the villagers offered us leaves of Lemon Grass and we were advised to crush them and rub them over our limbs — a natural insect repellent!

Mosquitoes are quickly forgotten when you encounter the more exotic and lovely inhabitants of Ubin. The screeching calls and tail silhouettes of the Long-tailed Parakeets, their vivid green bodies, bright pink cheek patches and trailing tails are etched in my memory. Imagine seeing native parrots in Singapore and flocks of them! I was delirious! I have also stumbled upon a dead tree where a Oriental Magpie Robin was nesting — a rare encounter. But Jungle-fowl are common.

The presence of the Collared Kingfisher is unmistakable for its boisterous calls can be heard from afar. The Straw-headed Bulbul's bubbly calls are a prelude to the morning symphony of sounds. The Common Flameback's calls are quite shrill. Perched on a trunk, it nods its head in quick successions as it hammers its formidable beak into the bark once there are indications of insect-life — its hooded head and the unusual colours are quite a sight. This large woodpecker can be oblivious to visitors when it is feeding on insects. The Common Flameback is not as common as its name suggests and that is also true for many of the birds in Singapore that were once named "common".

Walking around Ubin at night can be delightful. During a vertebrate survey organised by the National Parks Board, I had the opportunity to view the Collared-scops Owl. A Common Palm Civet ran

Right: Although not as spectacular as its counterpart, the female Common Flameback (*Dinopium javanense*) still strikes an impressive figure.

Below left: The White-bellied Fish-eagle. One is often awed by the size and graceful flight of this majestic bird. It once proudly adorned the $10,000 Singapore currency note.

Below right: The Long-tailed Parakeet (*Psittacula longicauda*) is a common sighting and one is often drawn to the high-pitched screeching. Travelling in flocks of 10 to 20, its distinctive long pointed tail during flight is the means of identification. On closer view, its reddish head and green body is impressive.

frantically up amongst the clumps of coconuts as our torches caught its eye-glow and continued to stay away from view. Two Wood Owls were spotted during one of our night trips to the island. The distinctive calls allowed us to pinpoint their location and the adult bird snarled at us for turning our lights at it and also to protect its fledgling.

Watch out for a low-flying bird that takes off suddenly from the ground. It is the size of a pigeon with shining green feathers, and it usually lands further into the thickets. The Emerald Dove is such a beautiful bird. When I saw one in a cage at a resident's home, I felt very weighed down as not many people can appreciate nature as it is.

While watching the nesting White-bellied Fish-eagles, I was fortunate to stand among Pandan trees and luxuriate in the fragrance of their huge leaves, traditionally used to wrap rice dumplings. And if the Fish-eagle happened to glide low, just above these huge leaves, a watcher would realise how massive the bird's wingspan was.

Another large bird that had many bird-watchers excited was the Southern Pied Hornbill. I have watched the disbelief on visitors' faces as the hornbills glided in formation not too high above their heads.

A boat trip around the island is another high point in my Ubin memories. The constant gliding of a pair of Brahminy Kites at the beach told me that

Below: A common bird in the past, the population of Oriental Magpie (*Copsychus saularis*) plummeted due to its popularity as pets. Its melodious calls are music to the ears. However, small numbers have established themselves on the island.

Left: Once extinct in Singapore, the Southern Pied Hornbill (*Anthracoceros albirostris*) is making a comeback on Ubin. So far, a flock of nine has been recorded. It is sensitive to human intrusion during the initial stages of nest-building and is known to abandon its nest. The slow, laboured flight of these huge birds is a spectacle only the fortunate have witnessed.

17

the roar from the boat engines had disturbed their nesting. Grey Herons were easily spotted sunning themselves. The many Terns (Great Crested Tern, Lesser Crested Tern and Black-naped Tern) that stood firmly on the *kelong* poles despite the boat's proximity had all the photographers scrambling for their cameras.

Lush stands of mangrove plants still fringe the river mouth and parts of the coast. The clear sand at some spots certainly looks irresistible to sunbathers.

Anglers can expect a reasonable haul as the mangroves are home to many species of fish. At the estuary, some anglers dig for sea-worms. These bait worms have centipede-like legs and they bite.

At the Noordin Beach campsite, I once saw two teenaged boys taking aim with catapults at a poor sunbird flitting in the beach vegetation. For some to appreciate nature, it must lie cradled within their hands — dead or alive. The boys did not seem to appreciate friendly advice. Sadly, on my way out,

Right: Seaweed (*Ulva* sp.) dangles on the arched roots of the *Rhizophora* sp., the shore carpeted with its luxuriant growth. This is an unusual sight in Singapore. A lush growth of mangrove forest still lines part of Ubin's coast and estuarine habitats. A threatened but important specialised ecosystem, the mangrove forests are the intermediary between the sea and land. The unique flora and fauna is often unappreciated as mangroves are less accessible. The plants have breathing roots that jut out from the mud or appear from branches or trunks which also help to support the plant. Seeds that are fertilised grow on the plant initially, sprouting roots and shoots before dropping off to anchor in the poorly aerated soils. The high salinity does not pose problems to these plants as they are able to filter out salt at the root level and some is excreted through special glands on leaves.

I found catapults sold at Ubin Village.

The breathtaking view from Puaka Hill is akin to being on the top of the world. On a clear day, you probably could see forever. The Puaka hilltop overlooks the Ubin Granite Quarry and standing by the edge of the quarry can be a scary experience. On one visit, I encountered the rare Stinkhorn fungus at the summit. It was sheer ecstasy.

The quarries are closed to the public now. I used to sit by the edge of the Ho Man Choo Granite Quarry, mesmerised by the jade-green waters. In the late afternoon, the sunlight's angle on the walls lit up the different shades of granite in hues of brown and ochre.

I could not resist the temptation to wade in the waters of the HDB Granite Quarry. I was surprised to find two fish species in the lake — the pretty Harle-

Above: The bright blue hind wings of the male Blue Pansy (*Junonia orithya*) is a beautiful sight. It is often seen on patches of grassland.

Left: With its white belly up, the straightened length of the Painted Bronzeback (*Dendrelaphis pictus*) looks like a fallen twig until it turns over. This is probably to avoid predation by eagles. In this picture, a frog looks doomed as the snake attempts to prevent it from breathing. This must have gone on for hours until our interruption and the snake suddenly released its grip. The frog managed to swim a little — still shaking off the effects of its epic struggle.

quin Rasboras and the Tiger Barbs. In my childhood, I used to catch fishes like these in streams, but in the quarry I no longer felt the need to capture them.

One memory in particular stands out. A group of visually handicapped people in rapturous spirits after having their senses excited by the "Sensory Trail" made me wonder how much we sighted people take all that we have for granted. Feeling the sea breeze, away from the fast-paced life of the city. Feeling the

texture of jackfruits and their leaves. Smelling the pandan and curry leaves. Scooping up well water and enjoying its coolness. Walking between banana trees, fingers brushing the trunks.

The fruits of Ubin are another part of its magic. The luscious, translucent, red Water Apple or *jambu air* fruits are dome-shaped, with a light texture. Another species is more cylindrically shaped and more opaque in texture. The flowers are bright red

Right: The Slender Pitcher Plant (*Nepenthes gracilis*) is found at the HDB and Ubin Granite Quarries. The plant is able to thrive on nutrient-poor soils. Insects drowned in the pitchers provide the nitrogenous compounds necessary for its growth. The pitchers often evoke expressions of awe. The chance to view these uncommon and unusual plants is itself a memorable experience.

Far right: A Fig tree (*Ficus* sp.) with a cluster of fruits. Pollination is most unusual in figs as flowers are contained within the fruit where tiny wasps bore into the fruit to fertilise them.

and young fruits are creamy, maturing red. Old coconuts that have just begun to sprout a sapling are my favourite. When cleaved with a parang the embryo within can be eaten. Yellowish on the outside and white inside, it has a mild sweet taste and light crunchy texture.

The huge jackfruits were tempting and with the residents resettled on the mainland, many of these fruits were just waiting to be harvested. I saw too, the exhilarated smiles on those who were fortunate enough to pick the fallen durians. Before the residents were resettled, durian season meant keeping vigilant watch against trespassers and one could feel the residents' searing gaze.

Fruits are not the only lure. Some of the restaurants on Ubin served wild boar meat too. Wild boars are rather secretive and it is not easy spotting one. I remembered an adult boar that sprinted across a trail when my son was cycling and he was pleasantly surprised at the rare experience. I had the good fortune of having a young boar pointed out to me. It had body streaks like that of a tapir but of a different colour — brown body with dark brown streaks. It was stranded up on an incline in a quarry and fortunately its parent was away foraging for food. After a few snapshots, I wasted no time getting away, fully aware that an adult boar can charge and inflict fatal injuries when cornered or when it wishes to protect its young.

Above: Coconuts galore. Coconut trees grow well all over the island. The taller trees are sometimes hit by lightning while many have their leaves destroyed by adult Rhinoceros Beetles (*Oryctes rhinoceros*). The fallen nuts sprout easily.

Left: Prized and much sought after — "Ubin's durians". These trees are the last few found in Singapore. Some of the fruits were creamy yellow and I could have sworn they tasted like the highly acclaimed D24 durians from Malaysia.

Reflection

Ten years back, Pulau Ubin was still relatively undisturbed except for the sudden roar of the badly maintained motorcycles and gush of diesel smoke from taxis that obviously looked destined for the junkyard. Presently, congestion at Ubin Village is due to increasing numbers of visitors. But away from the town centre, the sense of tranquillity is still pervasive.

However, the quaint and simple homes, the uncomplicated and serene lives the residents chose, will sadly be missed. I could still swivel on an ancient barber's chair in one of the Malay homes where once haircuts were readily dispensed. Now, hurricane and pressure lamps lie rusted in a rubbish pile. These lamps were once commonly used for lighting.

I still look forward to escape to my favourite haunt from my daily stresses. Left in its original state, Ubin will continue to surprise me. The rustic peace, chirping and free flying birds, the wilderness and the laid-back lifestyle — a trip to the island is a soul-searching experience, one that is filled with nostalgia. The classic Malay and Chinese architecture and the people who helped give Ubin its charms are unique in modern Singapore. But changes are beginning to take its toll on the idyllic island.

I am not too sure where else to retreat for some simple pleasures in life. I had previously not known what lived beyond the trees. Pulau Ubin has changed

Left: Metal worked by the hands of man might conquer nature for a while, but eventually, time and nature prevail, as this rusting lorry on Ubin shows.

23

the way I look at life. It has become my sanctuary. When I heard that Bin Kiang School was demolished recently, my heart cried out. An important landmark completely obliterated. Was it the beginning of the end of Ubin?

At the jetty, boats wait to bring visitors back to the mainland. I look at the quaint coffee shop of Encik Ali bin Montail and realise that a huge Tamarind tree straddles a granite rock next to his shop and that I had missed it until I tried to look beyond the obvious. As I walk towards the jetty, I pause and stare at the granite rock, for it resembles the profile of a rhinoceros. Like the rhinoceros that is nearly extinct, Pulau Ubin, an island so unlike the mainland, may also be but a memory. Like the rich changing colours of the kaleidoscope, the island has only intense memories for me.

The call of Ubin sounds more like a whisper now.

Right: Aerial view of the jetty and the town centre. The Community Centre is situated on the lower left with a light blue roof. An upgraded jetty on the right facilitates access to this rural retreat. Floating fish cages in the background are insufficient to meet the increasing demands for fresh seafood.

Left: A view of the jetty from the road outside the Information Kiosk at Ubin Village.

Above: Finding solace amidst splashing waves. Exquisitely carved over a long time, this granite rock serves as a reminder of the island's land composition.

25

THE STONE ISLAND

Pulau Ubin is composed of igneous rocks of granite that are believed to be more than 200 million years old. The island was transformed when the land masses were drowned by water. A core of granite rock withstood the ravages of weather and to this day, lies northeast of mainland Singapore.

Boomerang-shaped, Ubin is about 8 km at its greatest length and varies from 1.3 to 1.7 km at its breadth. With an area of 1,020 hectares (10.2 sq km), the island was left underdeveloped until recently. Pulau Ubin lies in the Straits of Johor and is separated from mainland Singapore by the Serangoon Harbour.

The Malays called the island Pulau Batu Ubin or Granite Stone Island. The rocks on the island were used to make floor tiles and were called "Jubin", which was then shortened to Ubin. A resident remembered a map in which the British named it "Woman's Island", probably due to the way it was pronounced and translated into English.[1] Two islets, Pulau Sekudu (southeast of Ubin) and Pulau Ketam (southwest) are part of Ubin.

Above right and opposite: Painting by John Turnbull Thomson, 1850. A recent photograph, 150 years later, of the same fluted granite boulder with an overgrown fig tree.

Left: Fashioned by the changing tide and vagaries of weather, a granite rock (left of picture) resembling the profile of a frog sticks out of the water south of Ubin. Not surprisingly, the whole group of rocks is referred to as Frog Island or Pulau Sekudu.

Undulating with low hills and valleys, small rivers traverse the terrain in many areas. Meandering rivers such as Sungei Besar and Sungei Mamam penetrate the island in the north whilst Sungei Jelutong and Sungei Puaka, the south. The highest point is the well-hidden Puaka Hill, rising 74 m above sea-level. Granite hills and mangrove swamps are scattered over the island which is surrounded by narrow stretches of sandy, muddy as well as rocky beaches. *Kelong* (a series of poles inserted on the seabed that help guide fishes to an area where nets can be hoisted) and floating fish farms are concentrated on the northern and southeastern part of the island.

Preceding spread and below: Coastal view of Ubin Village and wooden jetty. To reach the steps on the jetty, one often has to step over mooring ropes and hop from boat to boat. In the past, one had to step ashore on sand or mud depending on the tide.

Human settlement

Encik Endut Senin was the founder of Kampung Surau. He came from Kampung Kallang (a settlement around the Kallang River) and sought the Sultan's approval (at Kampung Glam Palace) for abode on an island that had no name. Initially, Endut Senin planted padi and tapioca and took to fishing.

Others followed when they heard of his rich harvests from farming and fishing. About 50 Malay families joined him to make Pulau Ubin their home. Kampung Melayu (Malay Village) grew to become a thriving Malay community.

The Chinese were likewise lured to the island and soon 25 families settled there.[2] The Malay community congregated mainly at Kampung Melayu, Kampung Sungei Durian and Kampung Surau. Being fishermen, they tend to stay along the coasts. The Chinese were more involved in businesses and were drawn to Ubin Village (the town centre) and Kampung Jelutong. They also spread out all over the island, setting up home near major tracks, granite quarries and plantations. Other known villages were Kampung Che Jevah, Kampung Noordin, Kampung Bahru and Kampung Tengah.

Mr Lim Chye Joo, the headman of Pulau Ubin, recalled the times when new arrivals bore the resentment of those already there. The Teochews and Hokkiens often clashed with each other until the arrival of the Japanese soldiers in World War II

when the two dialect groups declared themselves as Chinese. The bickering stopped thereafter.[3]

The Malays got on well with the Chinese and the only tense occasions were the racial riots in 1964, but fortunately there were no incidents in Ubin. The Chinese made sure they attended the Malay weddings on the island while the Malays attended the stage shows during the Lunar seventh month although they may not have understood most of it.[4]

Triads began to appear, extorting money from merchants and quarry bosses. There were two main triads on the island and a resident referred to them as the "second government".[5]

A population census in 1970 reported 2,028 residents (Chinese 1,599, Malays 411, Indians 15 and others three) and of which 1,083 were males and 945 females. As many as 45 residents found it necessary to commute regularly to the mainland to work. At the time, the island also supported six provision shops, three coffee shops, two barber shops, a motorcycle cum bicycle repair shop, a drug store and even a bookshop. It was a hive of activity. Near the *wayang* stage in Ubin Village, roadside hawkers did a roaring business.[6]

Above left: A *kampung* dwelling. Living near each other has its advantages: there is opportunity for greater interaction and sharing of resources.

Above right: These womenfolk at the Malay Village sort and clean the fishes and Flower Crabs caught by the fishermen. Although not as meaty as the mud crabs, these crabs rank very high for taste.

Left: Ubin Village has had a predominantly Chinese population, with business as their forte. Today, bicycle rental is big business on Ubin. It's the most practical form of transport on the island.

31

Quarrying

The first granite quarry was discovered before 1848 and quarrying works began after that. At that time, granite was ferried for the building of the Horsburgh Lighthouse. The Pedra Branca (or "White Rock"), located 56 km east of Singapore, was found to be dangerous to shipping. It was resolved in 1836 that the rock be marked by a lighthouse to be named after Captain James Horsburgh (an eminent hydrographer).

John Turnbull Thomson built the lighthouse initially with bricks and mortar in 1847, only to see it being washed away. Granite from Ubin Island was found to be more suitable. Thomson engaged a workforce of skilled stone breakers and stone cutters on the island to fashion the granite for the lighthouse. These blocks were numbered and grooved to fit in their final position on location at the lighthouse. The vicinity around the rock was notorious for pirate attacks and as the blocks were transported by *tongkang* (lighters), they had to be escorted by gunboats. The lighthouse was completed in 1851. The Raffles Lighthouse, marking the southernmost tip of Singapore territory, was also built using granite from Ubin.

Migrant workers converged on Ubin as there was work to be done. But quarry work was hard as it was carried out manually with hand tools, unlike the more recent practice of using explosives. Larger scale quarrying by the British necessitated the influx of Chinese labourers. Pulau Ubin became a major supplier of granite for the building industry. Whilst most of the workers were Chinese, cottage industries selling polished granite slabs, stone tombs and granite grinders by Malays were popular. The Malays had a method of hewing and treating the granite, enabling slabs of it to be cut.

In the 1990s, Aik Hwa Granite Quarry was producing 160 to 180 tonnes of granite per month and at one time was supplying about 30 to 40 per cent of the mainland's requirement. The quarry once employed more than 100 workers and most of them were residents of Ubin. The granite was processed

Below: Chinese stonecutters at work on the Pulau Ubin Quarry, as seen from a painting by J. T. Thomson, 1851. Granite was cut up into blocks for construction of the Horsburgh Lighthouse.

Right: For years villagers had been talking about a pair of Tapirs (*Tapirus indicus*) in Ubin. Only after a photograph taken in 1986 surfaced recently then it became apparent that it was not a myth after all. This dead Tapir fell off the cliff at the Ubin Granite Quarry and was subsequently buried there. Its partner probably perished on the island. Here a worker poses with a raised wooden stick.

by a number of crushers (primary, secondary and tertiary) to suitable sizes. The crushers were connected by a series of conveyor belts.

The most popular granite size was 2 cm, commonly used for mixing with concrete. For reclamation works, 23 cm size was needed. Retaining walls needed 15 to 23 cm, roads needed 5 cm and granite "dust" (5 mm) was mixed with concrete. Also known as "manufactured sand", granite dust makes very consistent concrete. Lung damage was a major risk in quarry works and about 10 to 20 per cent of workers succumbed to this. Loss of hearing was not uncommon when explosives were used. The provision and use of face masks and earplugs were not strictly enforced then. In the early 1990s, automation reduced the workforce and also reduced the exposure. Control towers with air-conditioning and air-conditioned lorries reduced the problems of dust contamination. At one time, there were five granite quarry operators. All quarrying works have ceased.

Agriculture

The lush tropical forest was left undisturbed and the waters around the island were pristine and the shores devoid of rubbish, until the influx of workers and land clearing for plantations began. Rubber was first introduced to Singapore in 1877 and only after H.N. Ridley had found improved means of tapping the latex, did the rubber tree become a popular plantation crop. Vast areas in the east were devoted to its planting and to this day, its many trees remain.

Rubber tapping ceased in the 1980s when it was no longer viable due to increasing costs of production as compared to other countries. Fruit orchards of durians, rambutans, jackfruit and papaya were popular among residents. Coconut plantations did not need much attention and were a popular choice. Demand for orchid, pandan and jasmine encouraged residents to plant them as cash crops. Cultivation of orchids started around 1970, but the large farms were unsuccessful and had to cease operations. Only two small orchid farms are still running.

Above, top and bottom: Old rubber plantations still stand. These trees are reminders of the heyday of the booming rubber industry. They provide excellent shade along some trails. Brown streaked seeds litter the floor and are popularly collected as souvenirs.

Right: Drying rubber sheets at Kampung Che Jevah when rubber production was still a viable business in Singapore.

Far right: One of the last of the durian trees still found in Singapore.

Left: Prawn farming. Ropes were used to bisect the nets and one end of the rope was hauled up using a pulley system. The prawns were driven to a corner where marketable sizes were scooped up for sale.

Fishing

Seafood is a popular choice for many Singaporeans and it was not surprising that fish farms and *kelong* around the island flourished. The Agri-food and Veterinary Authority of Singapore helped fish farmers to develop their fish and green mussel farms.[7]

Prawn farms making use of the tidal waters of the mangrove swamps thrived in Ubin whilst reclamation works on the mainland reduced the viability of prawn farming. During the period from 1954 to 1959, the government opened up 120 hectares of land for prawn farming[8] and this was quite lucrative as large prawns fetched about $20 to $25 a kati (0.7 kg) then.

Fed on algal growth and prawn-feed, the prawns were harvested at night to be sold to middlemen during the wee hours of the morning. Freshwater ponds were often stocked with Common Snakeheads and Giant Snakeheads. Residents became more self-sufficient and less reliant on the mainland for their food.

Above and below right: Bin Kiang School and the graduation photograph of a primary class in 1969 (the 18th class to graduate). For those born in Pulau Ubin, Bin Kiang School was the only school on the island, but it was more convenient than travelling to the mainland.

Below left: Report book from Bin Kiang School.

Infrastructure

Built by the Japanese between 1942 and 1943, the first jetty on Pulau Ubin eased travel to the island. Before that, one had to walk over the muddy shore to dry land.

During the Japanese attack on Singapore, the Imperial Guards (Kanoe Division) first landed on Pulau Ubin on 7 February 1942, after they had occupied Johor Bahru. From 9 February onwards, they proceeded to sweep through mainland Singapore.

Fearing for their safety, some residents built bomb shelters in anticipation of bombing raids. Remnants of these two tunnels are still present in two homes. But the Japanese left the folks in Pulau Ubin much alone.

After the war, a school was built in 1952 to cater to a growing population of children. Before that, the wayang stage served as a classroom. Bin Kiang School was built from funds raised by the resident Chinese community and once boasted about 400 students. The school's windows opened out to a patch of greenery where learning amidst the chirping of birds is an experience in nature itself. But the promise of industrialisation, new towns and modern amenities on the mainland lured many residents away from the simple life on Ubin. The school closed in 1985. After that, the building was used as a gathering point for activities for the aged.[9] On 2 April 2000, the school was demolished.

History is sketchy about the establishment of a private Malay school at Kampung Melayu but Encik Ali bin Montail remembered it to be around 1956. It was closed in the late 1970s as there were not enough pupils. At its peak, there were two classes with three teachers and 60 pupils. Sited on elevated land, there is now no trace of the Malay school.

A Maternity and Child Health Clinic (M&CH) was established on the island in 1957. A team of nurses visited the M&CH clinic two to three times a week

using boats from Changi Point. They attended to the needs of the expectant women, post-partum mothers and their children (up to pre-school) which include immunisations and treatment of minor ailments.

Deliveries were referred to the Kandang Kerbau Hospital. A midwife was stationed at the M&CH daily, during office hours, to attend to this group. She visited the residents at their homes for emergency deliveries and follow-up services. The clinic was closed down on 1 December 1987 when demand for its services dwindled. A seafood restaurant took over the site.

A new jetty was opened on 24 October 1965 by Mr Ong Pang Boon (then Minister of Education). With increasing human traffic, that jetty was inadequate for the island's needs. The jetty was upgraded (which included a shelter and a seating area) at a cost of $400,000 and declared open by Mr Teo Chong Tee (MP for Changi Constituency) on 10 December 1994.

Overlooking the Serangoon Harbour, the Pulau Ubin Community Centre is a meeting point for Ubin's residents. This was a far cry from the zinc and wooden structure built in 1961.[10] Originally it was a commu-

Above: Mr Lee Kuan Yew, Singapore's then Prime Minister, visited the island on 15 November 1964.

Other residents had to travel to the Somapah Outpatient Clinic for their medical problems. The police post was often contacted for emergencies. Officers at the post would in turn contact the marine police to transport the victims to the mainland. According to residents, the M&CH site used to be a remand centre for the Japanese and after the war, it served as an opium retail shop.

nity hall built with contributions from residents, but in 1966, it was converted to a community centre.

This centre was a hub of activities and had a kindergarten class too. The screening of movies at the basketball court was an activity highlight, often drawing two to three hundred residents.

The community centre was renovated in 1993 at a cost of $20,000.[11] A dinner to celebrate 25 years of

Above left: Maternity & Child Health Clinic. Due to a declining population, the building was demolished when it no longer served its purpose. It was replaced by a seafood restaurant.

Above right: The opening of the main jetty by Mr Ong Pang Boon in 1965 was a milestone in the history of the island. Greater accessibility allowed more people to appreciate its treasures.

nation building was held at the basketball court and about 500 residents turned up for the grand bash.[12] Now, only groups of visitors rendezvous at the basketball court before they set out for their trips across Ubin.

Campsites

Pulau Ubin was an ideal site for the Singapore Outward Bound School, established in 1967 by Dr Goh Keng Swee. Renamed Outward Bound Singapore (OBS), its management was transferred from the Ministry of Defence to the People's Association in 1991.

The popularity of its programmes required that its premises be enlarged to meet demand. The new centre was officially opened on 27 September 1997 by Prime Minister Goh Chok Tong (who is also Chairman of the People's Association). OBS has a built-up area of 66,200 square metres.

Above: View of the Community Centre. It has a reading lounge with newspapers, an office, a room with a table-tennis table and a patio that opens up to the sea. These days, more visitors than residents use the centre.

Right: Teamwork at Outward Bound Singapore, located on the western end of Ubin. Building a "rugged society" has long been one of Singapore's aims.

"If we are not rugged, fit and healthy as a society, we will not be able to withstand the pressure of competition, endure the rigours of military training and survive the heat of battles."

— Mr Goh Chok Tong, the First Deputy Prime Minister (*The Straits Times*, 24 April 1990).

Even the National Police Cadet Corps (NPCC) is increasing the capacity of its campsite from 80 to 500 to cater to new demands. The new 30-hectare site between Kampung Noordin and Kampung Bahru includes adventure areas and obstacle courses.[13] Originally occupying a 0.88-hectare site at Kampung Bahru, the NPCC Campsite was officially opened on 19 September 1987 by Guest-of-Honour, Brigadier-General (Res) Tan Chin Tiong (Permanent Secretary, Home Affairs).

Leaving Ubin

But the exodus from Ubin started in the 1970s due to the closing down of the granite quarries. By 1980, only 1,242 residents remained and the population dwindled to about 400 by 1995. The last quarry, the Aik Hwa Granite Quarry, closed in 1999 just after the RDC (Resource Development Corporation) Quarry.

The resident's request for a power station for electrical supplies was turned down by the Public Utilities Board and the lack of ready supply of electricity and other basic amenities like running water and modern sewerage systems probably speeded the exodus. Land acquisition prevented developments by residents to their homes and compounds.

According to the Census of Population in 1990, there were less than 200 people living in Ubin then. A local press report put the number at around 250.[14] Many

Left: Coconuts trees and cyclists. Very few sites in Singapore can boast of coconut plantations and fruit orchards. Left unchanged, the island is a reflection of our forgotten rustic past. Pedal power is the main means of travel through the various habitats and sites and is something cycling enthusiasts revel in.

residents are retired, some still fish or farm and some own shops to serve the growing number of visitors.

After the obliteration of Pulau Sakeng for use as a landfill, Pulau Ubin remains the last bastion of Malay *kampung* life. Will Pulau Ubin be swallowed up like Pulau Sakeng? Already there are suggestions to link the mainland to Pulau Ubin by MRT. Ubin's rich past will be forgotten if a whole way of life is erased.

THE CULTURAL HERITAGE

Legend has it that Pulau Ubin was formed when three animals from Singapore (a frog, a pig and an elephant) challenged each other to a race to the shores of Johor. Whoever failed would turn into a rock. All three had difficulties. The elephant and pig together changed into Pulau Ubin whilst the frog became Pulau Sekudu or Frog Island.

From the explanation of the island's origins to the Chinese operas to the places of worship to the homes — and graves — of the people, Pulau Ubin is a rich, microcosmic concentration of Singapore's cultural heritage.

Rituals

A drum roll and a clash of cymbals announced the arrival of actors brilliantly garbed in traditional period costumes. The older folks sauntered to the front of the stage lugging plastic chairs. Children rushed in eager anticipation and curiosity, trying to get choice spots. Taxis meandered through the crowd, blasting their horns.

On stage, the drama was unfolding. A generator was working overtime to feed the electrical needs of the stage. The bare fluorescent tubes whitewashed some of the colours of the decorative side panels. The backdrop cleverly camouflaged the imperfections of the stage. The loudspeakers wailed and blared.

With fingers delicately poised, movements fleeting and intonation exaggerated, the actors spoke in singing tunes, accompanied by a motley crew of musicians on traditional instruments. The background props changed with

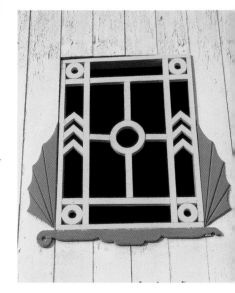

Opposite: Once the centre stage for education and activities, the Wayang House is a postwar structure in the main square of Pulau Ubin which faces directly the Chinese temple dedicated to the Taoist deity Da Bo Gong. Classical Teochew opera is performed on this stage during the birthday of the deity and the seventh month of the lunar calendar or the Festival of the Hungry Ghosts. In a 1988/89 report, architecture students from the National University of Singapore wrote: "The Wayang House stands regal and serene amidst the hustle and bustle of everyday life; it is a symbol of hope and prosperity for the people of Pulau Ubin."

Right: The carved windows of the Ubin Wayang House.

amateurish attempts but it was not supposed to be a "high-tech" show. Already, only the older people understood the opera, a part of our cultural heritage incrementally lost with every generation.

Opposite the Wayang House, some worshippers dipped the huge joss sticks in flammable liquid before lighting them up. These joss sticks were about 1.82 m in length and the urn could accommodate three joss sticks adequately. Red candles flickered and whiffs of smoke from the smaller joss sticks filled the air. Two empty oil drums, rusty and one end cut open, were used to burn the paper

offerings to the dead and the fire danced as the paper was tossed in.

The incense from the huge joss sticks reached the nostrils of worshippers. They chanted as they planted the smaller joss sticks into the urns which were overflowing with ashes. The caretaker was dousing the candle flames and carefully laid the candles in a box to make way for more offerings. A monk blessed a worshipper, lightly touching her forehead as he chanted his blessings. The scented papers were burned and hurriedly brought to the red kiln before the flames could engulf their hands.

Opposite and above: Chinese opera at the Wayang House — once a popular recreation to while away the evening hours, the art faces dwindling audiences despite efforts to revive public interest. *Wayang* performances usually take place during religious festivals.

Following pages, left and right: Devotees at the Da Bo Gong Temple making offerings.

Worship

The two Thai Buddhist temples in the north near the HDB Granite Quarry attract a number of worshippers during the weekend. Supplications are mumbled in tones only the immortals can hear. The mantras are more audible as the saffron-robed priests chant in unison. The tortoise shell was tapped at the start of prayers; a haunting rhythm that seems predictable and melodic.

Opposite the headman's house nearer the mangrove forests is yet another Thai Buddhist temple. Inside the temple, the statue of Buddha is in immaculate condition.

Towards the northeast coast near the RDC Quarry, a small Taoist shrine painted all yellow is surrounded by plants, dominated by yellow bamboo. Inside, on the granite altar, is a framed deity also in yellow. The walls are yellow too. It was not unusual for shrines to be located near the quarry sites as workers often prayed for their safety and sought blessings.

There is also the story of a German girl who accidentally fell off a steep cliff whilst running away from the British who had come to take over the plantation on August 1914 (her father was a plantation manager). That was when World War I was declared.

Her remains were once kept in a shrine on the hill adjacent to the Aik Hwa Granite Quarry but all that disappeared.[15] The shrine of the German girl was once popular amongst gamblers.

Right and below right: Devotees at the Thai temple. Crowds throng the temple during religious festivals and Ubin's battered taxis are in great demand on those days.

Below left: Shrines are scattered all over the island. Located near Tajam buoy (OBS) this once immensely popular shrine was accessible from the sea. Old photographs showed the jetty and platform. Now only parts of the jetty remain.

Opposite: This shrine at Aik Hwa Granite Quarry was supposed to house the remains of a German girl who perished during World War I. It was once popular as it was said to bring luck to gamblers.

In the southeastern part of Ubin, a mosque faces the sea. It resembles a *kampung* house except for the crescent on the roof. Inside, mats are laid on the floor and five clocks show the different prayer times.

Seven temples, eight shrines and one mosque scattered all over the island may seem a little excessive for the population of Ubin, even at its peak, but the influx of worshippers during religious festivals indicate their popularity. For those in search of spiritual fulfilment, distance is not a deterrent. Taxis are available to all places of worship.

Graves

People were born on Ubin. People lived, worked and played there. And many were laid to rest on their beloved island.

There were three locations where the Chinese were buried. Towards the west, just before the Thai temple, about 35 mostly Cantonese residents are buried. Frangipani, Rubber and Albizia trees provide shelter for the long departed. Dollarbirds and Yellow-vented Bulbuls cry in the vicinity.

Relatives visit the graveyards during Ch'ing Ming (All Souls' Day) to pay their respects to the dead. Some appear to have been neglected or forgotten. Some had elaborate designs and some were simple, flat slab tombstones. Many were buried in the 70s and some

did not have any photographs on the tombstones.

Behind the police post, lie the graves of men who were killed in clan-based clashes. They were unceremoniously buried and the granite tombstones marked their untimely demise. Few people know of its existence for the inscriptions (these were painted over instead of carved) were barely visible and there were no raised tombs — only flat ground.

A larger graveyard is opposite the main gate to Ho Man Choo Granite Quarry and on a side path before the path leading to Noordin Beach. It contains about 70 burial sites.

At the mosque by the sea, paired, simple, sculptured granite tombstones (*batu nisan*) are scattered at the back of the building. These lie amidst some tall forest trees; the larger tombstone of the pair depicts the cranial region. As the face should face Mecca, the pair of tombstones are aligned in the east-west direction; the larger tombstone faces the smaller towards the west.

A more remote graveyard (or *kubor* in Malay), lies away from the main trails, on elevated land and beyond the site of the former Malay School. At least 50 burial plots were noted; some had cloth covering the granite tombstones and some of these were made of wood but they were generally unmarked. Some tombstones were also found around the homes at Kampung Melayu.

Below: In the past, the tombstones had simple inscriptions and were less elaborate.

Opposite: Well shaded and within sniff from the sea breeze, Muslims were laid to rest behind the Mosque. Scattered tombstones marked the burial sites.

Dwellings

The early settlers were Malay fishermen who used to fashion their fishing boats (*jong*) from solid tree trunks where the pulp was dug out. As some of their homes faced the sea, these homes had private jetties. Their homes had no fences; the clever use of potted plants defined the sense of territory. The open living styles promoted the spirit of cooperation or "gotong royong". Neighbours often shared their woes and blessings and they behaved like an extended family.

The Malay houses are found on the eastern part of the island. The houses are either built on raised platforms or on the ground. Usually a house is a combination of both. The raised platform allows for greater ventilation. Even the chickens and ducks need to escape the midday sun.

Like the Chinese houses, they are built on timber posts and have timber walls. Architecturally, there are major differences. Attap-thatched roofs (made from Nipah palm leaves) used to be common and have been converted to corrugated zinc roofs or clip-lock metal roofs.

Right: Former residents of Ubin returning to relax by the beach. This small pavilion stands almost next to the water's edge. With its raised platform, villagers and residents can take a break there with the breeze in their faces.

Opposite: A Malay home in classic Malay architectural style stands in an idyllic setting.

This spread: Typical *kampung* dwellings. Elevated, they avoid contact with the dirt from the ground and flooding from the adjacent mangrove. Some have large jars next to the steps (opposite, top left) for collecting rain water, used to clean one's feet before entering the home. The veranda is ideal for a tête-à-tête or just for watching the world pass by. Discarded hurricane lamps such as these (opposite, centre) can be seen on Pulau Ubin. Lack of electricity once necessitated the use of these lamps at night.

The casement windows have timber railings. Often, colourful curtains are parted at the centre and are secured at mid-length. The timber panel wall tops are laced with decorative timber grilles. The living rooms and master bedrooms are usually on raised platforms. The dining rooms, kitchens and toilets are built on the ground. Fruit trees and ornamental plants usually abound on the grounds. Chickens run freely and it is not surprising that these have relatively lower fat compared to mass-produced chickens.

Chinese houses line the roads of Ubin Village. These simple, wooden houses are also scattered throughout the western part of the island and have common characteristics. The walls are made of

This spread: Chinese homes — the entrance, living room and kitchen area. Generator power meant that residents could utilise simple luxuries like TVs and fans. These wooden homes were built in a short time and at minimal cost.

56

timber panel and the roofs of corrugated zinc with asbestos false ceilings.

The main entrance leads to a living room and altar and a wooden threshold at the entrance prevents dust from being swept into the cement screed floor. Wire-mesh grilles at the top of walls provide for ventilation, while cobwebs dangle on the wire-mesh.

Casement windows open outwards to a view of the courtyards. There are also wooden thresholds to the master bedrooms and some rooms have raised floors. Those at the town centre had been converted to eateries or shophouses storing bicycles for rental. The only two-storey wooden house on the island belongs to the headman and it speaks of the social status accorded to people of prominence.

Laid-back and undeveloped, generators provide electricity for some of the nocturnal lighting needs

Above: An Ubin kitchen. Unlike custom-made kitchen cabinets in modern homes, most of the utensils here are all within sight and easy reach.

of Ubin homes and the lack of piped water has not deterred the residents. The warm glow comes from filament bulbs but many have been replaced with fluorescent tubes. Pressure lamps were also handy once.

Nightfall is meant for early retirement although some homes are equipped with TV sets. Water is obtained from man-made wells and is a natural source of mineral water. These served the residents well until a recent drought.

A unique dwelling is a pre-war English cottage at No. 1 Pulau Ubin, which blends with the surrounding forest and is often missed when approached by land. To the left of the rear entrance is a small building, probably a guard room or store hut.

The facade faces a robust concrete jetty and from the sea, the magnificence of the building becomes more obvious. The black arched roofs and aged

rumble walls (granite blocks embedded in cement mortar joints) are distinctive.

The fireplace in the living room is a mystery — cold was never a problem in the tropics. The yellow-brown floor fronting the building is covered with algae. Towards the rear of the building is a patio with a roof covered with Nipah leaves and supported by coconut poles. This is probably a more recent addition. The building gives a commanding view of the sea and of Pulau Sekudu or Frog Island.

According to Professor Edmund Waller, the building is an example of English Lutyenesque architecture adapted to the tropical climate. The lodge was built between the 1920s and 1930s for a resident British medical officer for his vacations.

Encik Sulung bin Latiff mentioned that his father was the caretaker of the building and his grandfather tended the garden. The house was later owned by a rubber company and was the home of the local rubber estate manager.

Remembered in art

Besides naturalists, artists too, are mesmerised by the charms of the island. They draw inspiration from the undisturbed and the untamed, the old and the quaint, the serenity and the madness. Palettes of colour in one hand and brush in the other, hand movements are dictated by the urgency to capture their response to a scene.

The urgency is more pressing as one senses the inevitable — the invasion of Ubin for housing. For all of us, the past has important lessons and meanings for the present. Perhaps preserving some of these homes and the setting-up of a heritage trail will help us understand our roots better. Some of the homes at Ubin Village and Kampung Melayu could be retained for this.

Like mainland Singapore, Pulau Ubin's history has similar humble beginnings. But unlike the former, the lack of massive developments has been a blessing. Ubin evokes its own character but the focus is changing. There is a price to pay for what we call progress.

Opposite: Various views of the pre-war English cottage, No. 1, Pulau Ubin. This British-inspired bungalow is accessible from the sea by jetty. Still sitting pretty, the building has weathered years of neglect.

Above: A painting of the *wayang* at Ubin village by local artist Pang Teng Khoon captures an aspect of the island's rich heritage.

PORTRAITS OF A LIFESTYLE

While it is possible to appreciate the natural wonders of Pulau Ubin by exploring it, it is only through contact and conversation with the residents that the small details which make a lifestyle surface. And since many residents have lived on Ubin all their lives, a wealth of oral history awaits the researcher who wants to go beyond archives and artefacts.

Opposite: Boats docked by the wooden jetty at high tide. It is not unusual to see grounded boats being repaired during low tide.

Right: Pulau Ubin's coastal areas are important for fishing. Boathouses on the left of the jetty belong to fishermen who prefer to stay on water. The jetty leads to the Ma Chor Temple (on the right) which is a popular place of worship. Devotees usually arrive in boats from Punggol.

Below left: Large wasps or hornets (*Vespa* sp.) inflict vicious and at times fatal stings when their nests are disturbed. Fortunately some nests are built high on trees and are not easily provoked. Once detected, staff from NParks will attempt to destroy them by burning their nests. The public is thus better protected from potentially threatening situations.

Below right: Looking for the elusive tiger after a report by a resident, Cik Pungot Ahmad. Staff from NParks and sharpshooters from the Marine Police combed the whole island looking for possible indications of its presence.

A rough life?

Life on Ubin may seem a little easier these days, with staff from the National Parks Board patrolling the island and making it safer for all. They remove the nests of hazardous insects like wasps and hornets and make sure people stay out of the quarry lakes. They conduct guided walks and do research too. The Police Coast Guard are ever present, slowly cruising in their motorboats along the Straits of Johor and looking out for illegal immigrants.

In fact, Pulau Ubin only makes the news when something unusual and dramatic happens. A marauding elephant attacked a man whilst he was praying at a shrine.[16] The wild elephant was captured with much effort and had a warm send-off by more than 40 islanders.[17] Besides that, the search for four pirates who escaped to the island[18] and the elusive tiger[19] were anxious moments for most residents. The number of abandoned dogs[20] were too much to handle for the residents as the creatures drove them

up the wall with their incessant barking. Help from the SPCA (Society for the Prevention of Cruelty to Animals) helped solved the problem.

The exceptionally high tide,[21] a 25-year record, had waves lashing on the many roads on the island but some fish farm owners were also badly affected — they lost all their fish stock. Tragedy has also struck, with drowning accidents in the quarries and in the rivers, especially near the tidal gates.

The demands of daily life are also more difficult on Ubin. But the lack of water supply and electricity has not deterred residents. They have dug their own wells and invested in generators for electricity. However, during one particularly dry spell, the wells dried up and water from the mainland had to be brought in by barges.[22] The Singapore Armed Forces and Civil Defence Forces helped transport and distribute water to the residents.

Petrol is also precious on Ubin. There are no petrol kiosks and residents have to either carry in their own or buy small quantities from the sundry shops. These shops stock just about everything a householder, camper or visitor might need. Dried food, fresh food, fruits, fish, canned food, drinks, prayer paraphernalia — these shops at Ubin Village truly deserve to be called convenience stores.

Whatever the news that interests the mainland, there is a common thread — living so close to

Above: Generator — the life of Ubin. Lights, TV, fans and other basic electrical needs are served with a generator that runs on diesel. The contraption is noisy and the only way to silence the night is a gentle flick of a switch.

Left: A fellow nature lover, Sutari, demonstrating how to scoop water from an abandoned well. The pail had to be angled to cut into water before it could be scooped up. Lack of piped water has not deterred residents from making the best of their stay on the island. Water from artesian wells has supported the population of Ubin in the past.

nature, Ubin's people are more exposed to risks and inconveniences that someone living on the mainland would find most unnerving or uncomfortable. But in their choices — to live on Ubin, to persevere in barely viable occupations and to hold on to a lifestyle dear to them — these people demonstrate the strong need to be self-sufficient and the ability to simply take each day as it comes.

Above right: Living on borrowed time. Vehicles that would have been destined for the junkyard on the mainland still manage to ferry visitors about the island.

Right: The fruits of Ubin for sale at the village.

Opposite: Almost anything you want to eat or drink is available at the sundry shops. Even petrol can be purchased.

Farmers and fishermen

The first settlers on Pulau Ubin came because the farming and fishing were good. The crop and the catch were rich, more than enough to feed the families living on Ubin. Over a century later, some Ubin residents still farm and fish for their own food, but there have also been large commercial projects.

Mr Soh Boon Teck, 54, once reared tropical fish on the island. His farm is on the very remote Tanjung Balai (east) where he lived and worked for 13 years until recently, when the pet fish trade grew less viable. He now lives in Hougang, returning

Below: View from Puaka Hill. Less obvious and hidden from view from visitors are the fish and prawn farms. Residents are engaged in this trade as seafood is a lucrative business.

Left and following page: Mr Lim Eng Soon, 48, hauling his tropical fishes up for sorting before he sells them to the fish traders.

regularly on Sundays to tidy his farm. Old coconuts are harvested using a long pole with a sickle attached at the end and are transported by boat for sale to the mainland. He hopes to be compensated by the Government before he is resettled.

He remembers that sea bass used to be quite plentiful as they were easily caught at the beach but in the last ten years or so, the catch has been rather poor. Herds of wild boars are known to forage nightly around the farm and his dogs have been attacked by them. Despite the mosquitoes and sand flies, he wishes he could build a house by the sea and continue with his farming. These days, visiting his house during weekdays can be dangerous — his dogs are fed only once a week.

Mr Lim Eng Soon, 48, rents fish ponds from Mr Tang Hai Liang, another resident. Mr Lim travels by motorbike, ferrying fish feed he buys from the mainland. He has been rearing tropical fish since he was 10 years old. He started commercial fish farming in Jalan Kayu in mainland Singapore, but had to give up as he could not compete with bigger companies. With expertise only in this area, he started rearing tropical fish again in Ubin four years ago.

His solo operation is demanding and backbreaking, finishing late in the evenings every day. Nets are lowered into ponds delineated by plank walls. Once the fish fry have matured, they are transferred to these nets where they will grow until there

is a demand from the fish traders. Water for the ponds is siphoned from a well. When he lost his fish stock during the big flood in December 1999, it took him more than five months before he could start earning a profit again. But it has not deterred him. "This is the only trade I know and I will carry on as long as I can survive," he said in Hokkien.

I once watched prawn farmer Lee Chin Wah at work. Holding one end of a rope to bisect the prawn net, he pulled the rope up with a pulley, slowly driving the prawns into a corner. They were of marketable size, so he scooped up the prawns into an aerated container to be sold. The changing tide helped to prevent the waters from stagnating and he was also able to control it by damming the waters. A crab that was entangled in the net was mercilessly removed; it must have been siphoning food from the prawns. He ferried his catch on his motorbike to the middleman.

But these are actions Mr Lee no longer carries out, as he gave up the business in 1993. Mr Lee, 56, now works at a seafood restaurant on the island.

Life is also tough for the people who cultivate plants for a livelihood. Mr Lim Choo Gan is 57, the fifth son of Ubin's 94-year-old headman, Mr Lim Chye Joo. The younger Mr Lim is an orchid farmer.

At Mr Lim's farm, stalks of orchids are deftly cut twice a month and transported to the mainland to

Left: Mr Lim Choo Gan cutting his orchids for sale. Some of the orchids that you purchase from the mainland could have come from his farm.

be sold. The orchid farm is sited next to Mamam Beach. The elegant flowers of Dendrobium hybrids — purple and white — are popularly used in floral displays and they grow well on Ubin. He has been staying at this farm for 40 years, but has been in the orchid business for only 10.

His house is on the land leased from the Land Office and so far, he is happy to live there. He says the profit margin is marginal, so he supplements his income by selling cold drinks to visitors to the island.

Grunts from an enclosure reveal a trapped wild boar. Lacking tusks still, the mammal is a young three-year-old male Mr Lim rescued from his dogs. He says he was given a Leopard Cat, but released it

at the urging of members of the Nature Society of Singapore. Caged peafowls and Yellow-crested Cockatoos do not shy away from advertising their vocal prowess. The peacock in a courtship ritual made an impressive display of its tail feathers. Magpie Robins and Emerald Doves looked forlorn in their cages.

Mr Lim remembers fondly a young Buffy Fish Owl he nursed after it had fallen from a perch early in January 2000. He fed it with fish and mice during the day whilst its parents fed it at night. After two days, the bird was able to fly off with its parents.

The mangroves of Sungei Mamam are rich in fishes; the most common being the catfish and it was not surprising the owls chose that site to nest. Mr Lim kept his catch from the mangroves in nets in the river until needed. But he lost all the fish in the freak high tides of December 1999. The red snappers and groupers managed to escape with the rising waters. As the salt waters reached much higher ground, two of his durian trees also perished.

Fishing for one's own food is still possible, but it is no longer as viable on a commercial scale. I remember watching, in an earlier visit, the fishermen come in after a morning's work. As the sampans reached shore at the Malay Village, the boats needed to be dragged beyond the tidal line and tied. The fishes were carefully transferred. Sweat trickled from the bronzed and weather-beaten fishermen; it was just another day's work.

The *kampung* chicken, lean and mean, scuttled away at the sound of footsteps. The cocks flapped their wings with an air of arrogance. The chickens continued pecking the ground looking for bits of food. The scrap fish was kept for the chickens with the exception of the Puffer Fish. This was thrown back to the sea as it contained a deadly toxin. Discarded by the shore, a foot-long Estuarine Catfish wriggled, gasping for its last breath. Even when cooked, cats would rather starve than eat this fish. At low tide, the fisherman took the opportunity to caulk the leaks in their boats. Nylon nets were cleaned and hung on horizontal tree trunks to dry.

Like fishing, farming on Ubin may become less viable. And as potential sources of income dry up, residents will feel compelled to move to the mainland for better opportunities. But the space they leave behind will not be empty long.

Bikes, boats and cabs

A sign of the changing way of life on Ubin is the bicycle rental shop. Clearly targeted at Ubin's "tourist industry", these businesses are run by Chinese families, some of whom live on mainland Singapore, catching the first boat out to Ubin to open their shops. With more people visiting Ubin to experience the "Great Outdoors" by pedal power, more shops have sprung up over the years and competition has intensified. Bike rental ads are a jarring introduction to the visitor to Ubin. From $3/- to $15/- for a whole day (defined as the time you rent the bike till 6 pm that evening), the prices reflect the technical features of the bikes. You get options too. Extra cushion for the seats, a basket on the handle to hold your stuff or a baby seat: your wishes are easily fulfilled.

For the boatmen, life has not changed. The boatmen wait on the jetty, taking turns to make the run across Serangoon Harbour. They chat, drink coffee from cans that once contained condensed milk, and wait. On weekdays, the passengers are mostly islanders, moving their bags of tropical fish to the mainland,

Opposite, bottom left: Low tide is spent on maintenance of the boat. At Kampung Melayu, a fisherman caulked his boat to reduce water seepage. It is hard work toiling under the blazing sun.

Opposite, bottom right: Mr Ong Kay Sing at the helm. For the boatman, weekends are the best. The pace can be frantic as the hordes of visitors descend on Ubin to get away from the concrete jungle and seek solace in the rustic wilderness.

Left: Grime and mud. Pulau Ubin is one of the few areas in Singapore where mountain-biking can be taken to the limits. Naturally the bike business has flourished on the island. Competition means spanking new bikes and more thorough maintenance.

Right: Born in Ubin, Mr Ong Ah Lai would have preferred the island to remain undisturbed if given the choice. But the choice will not be his.

Below: A familiar face in Ubin, Mr Tea Tee Tee. There is this typical smile amongst Ubin's residents; seems they know something the mainlanders do not. Talk to them and they are ever willing to share their experiences.

or their catch of groupers. On weekends, the campers, anglers, hikers and bikers arrive in their droves.

Tanned and still youthful, Mr Ong Kay Sing, 49, started ferrying people by boat to Ubin more than 10 years ago. Born in Ubin, he has resettled in Pasir Ris. He once worked as a welder at one of Ubin's quarries.

Mr Ong Ah Lai, 50, was born in Kampung Bahru and had his primary education at Bin Kiang School. He proudly showed his school report book, kept for sentimental reasons. Red marks were interspersed with black, but that did not matter; for him, school was more like fun and play. He worked as a prawn pond operator before spending four years as a quarry blaster. He now lives in Tampines and returns daily to the island where he ferries workers to Outward Bound Singapore.

Like many of the older residents, he speaks fluent Malay. Saddened by the fact that many of his friends have also left the island, Mr Ong feels that there is no need to develop Pulau Ubin like Sentosa. He prefers Ubin to be less developed to preserve its rustic charm and *kampung* ambience. "Maintenance of the roads would be enough. Ubin attracts over a thousand visitors over the weekend. And one of the main attractions on the island is its birds," he said.

For the taxi driver, good roads are not enough to make a living. He needs passengers who want to travel some distance inland to the many places of worship on Ubin. The derelict taxis, some puffing enormous

Above: Taxi-stand at Ubin. For those who prefer to travel on the island with less sweat, taxis are available. Drivers don't need a driving licence on Ubin but this will soon change — from January 2001, the Road Traffic Act will come into operation in Ubin where all drivers would be required to have a valid driving licence.

clouds of black smoke, look recycled from the scrap-yards. Road tax is unheard of. At $18/- per taxi to the more distant destinations, drivers take turns to earn their living. Even then, it is only during the weekends and public holidays that they earn a decent income.

Mr Tea (Tay) Tee Tee, 58, moved to Ubin in 1983 when he set up a seafood business. It was closed down later as the Ministry of the Environment did not approve of some of the food outlets on the island. Mr Tea has been driving his taxi for the past eight years.

The demand for taxis started during 1990, when the Thai temple started to draw worshippers. The driv-ers are mainly residents of Ubin and life can be quite hard. Most weekdays, they earn less than $10 a day. He bought his used taxi for $3,000 (the Government does not allow any additional vehicles on the island).

Although he has a family in the mainland, he prefers to live on the island, going back once or twice a week to see them. He just cannot bear to leave and his best moments are with his friends on the tranquil island. His most memorable encounter was with a 40-kg python a year ago that was groggy after downing a duck. Construction workers promptly slaughtered the snake and had a feast.

Right: Encik Ali bin Montail makes *teh tarik* on request. The hot tea served is thus frothy and slightly cooled. Here he takes a breather before another boatload of visitors makes a beeline for his shop (above right) to taste his *lontong*. His shop is the first building to greet visitors to the island. A quick bite and drink — before one sets off to be absorbed by the ambience of Ubin.

Coffee, tea or mee

Just after the jetty, one cannot miss Encik Ali bin Montail's "Marine Coffeeshop". The stall has been around for 30 years. His shop has been dishing out *mee rebus*, *mee siam* and *lontong* for residents and visitors alike. Many visitors rave about his *lontong*.

Encik Ali, 69, was born in Kampung Melayu and spent much of his childhood in Ubin. He started work on the mainland, only to return to live and work on the island in 1965. He retired at 50 and managed his coffee shop thereafter. Like the headman, Mr Lim Chye Joo, Encik Ali is well respected, and very much involved in community service. He is the vice-chairman of the Community Centre Management Committee. His long service certificates adorn the wooden walls of his stall. Married, he is blessed with seven children.

Visitors to the island need not suffer from dehydration once out of Ubin Village. A few residents have set up little drinks stalls on Ubin and one example is Sulung's Coffeeshop at Kampung Melayu. Born on the island in 1932, Encik Sulung bin Latiff worked as a sprayer at the mosquito vector control unit with the British Royal Air Force before setting up his stall in 1976.

Like many of his neighbours, Mr Sulung lives on the mainland, returning to his stall during the weekends where about 250 to 300 visitors patronise his stall for drinks and *mee goreng*. He used to plant betel-nut, coconut, rubber and fruit trees and yearns to farm vegetables. Kampung Melayu is now left with 13 to 15 families, a far cry from more than 50 in the island's heyday.

Left: Checkers — A favourite intellectual pastime among the folks at Ubin. In between serving drinks, Encik Sulung bin Latiff takes time to socialise with a friend, Encik Ahmad bin Kassim, with a game or two.

鳥敬島村長兼
聯絡所主席
林再有BBM先生 惠存

精神可嘉

鳥敬島佛山亭中元會
爐主 李興光
敬贈
1999

有嘉業績耀乾坤

有福有祿壽千秋

再接再勵業昌盛

四代同堂留影

18

The Headman

One man who lived in Ubin through the island's "golden age" in the middle of the 20th century, is Mr Lim Chye Joo, Ubin's incumbent headman. He arrived in Ubin in 1936 at the age of 30. He had left his young wife and two sons in Swatow, China, to find his fortune on a little island off Singapore. He laboured hard on vegetable and chicken farms, earning a bit more from toiling under the scorching sun at the quarries. His work paid off. Within a year, he could send for his wife and sons.

The family grew. The Lims had six more sons and a daughter, but Mr Lim's wife, Madam Tan Ah Yew, died tragically at the age of 50. She was shot while trying to protect her family during a robbery.[23] The hole made by the bullet is still in the ceiling of their home.

Now retired from his last occupation as a shopkeeper-cum-trader, Mr Lim welcomes visitors to his home, as many are curious to look at some of the wildlife of Ubin that Mr Lim keeps in a private menagerie. Serving strangers Chinese tea in dainty traditional cups, Mr Lim is the perfect host, still deeply respected as Ubin Village's Headman — or "Dato", as the Malay villagers like to call him.

That respect has come from a lifetime of community service. Not happy that the *wayang* stage was used as a classroom, he soon gathered some friends

Left: The mementos of Mr Lim Chye Joo's accomplishments are exhibited outside the wall of his home. Every visitor is his friend. Drop in for a brief hello and he will reach out to shake your hand. Old age has hampered his movement, but he still chats with his friends from his trusty wheelchair.

Following page, top: The interior of Mr Lim's home. Portraits of his wife and ancestors face the entrance. His many children and grandchildren still share this dwelling. Amidst the clutter of the interior, the occasional clatter of the kitchen and angry growls from the underpowered motorbikes — a sense of perpetual calm pervades his home.

to help build the Bin Kiang School in the 1950s. The school closed in 1985 but not before recording a once high of 380 students and 11 teachers.

Mr Lim is the longest serving Chairman of the Community Centre Management Committee in the history of the People's Association. He is also the oldest Chairman of the oldest Community Centre.[24] For his dedication in community service, he was bestowed a BBM award in 1970 by the then President Benjamin Sheares.

Another Ubin pioneer is Mr Tang Hai Liang, also 94, who came from Canton, China. When the Japanese occupied Singapore in 1942, he decided that Pulau Ubin was a safer place to stay. He married (had three boys and two girls) and set up a sundry shop. He has been living on the island for the past 65 years.

A friend of Mr Lim, the headman, Mr Tang was also active in community work and was a member of the team that set up Bin Kiang School. He no longer runs a sundry shop, but tends to his plot of land, gardening and cutting grass. He lived briefly on the mainland but he knew his heart belonged to Ubin.

Ubin's young ones

The temple just after Jelutong Bridge attracts a crowd on Sundays. Miss Wong Siow Kian, 33, helps to upkeep the temple, which is next to her home. Initially it was a shrine but soon a temple was built

Right: Like many, reading the newspaper is a morning ritual for Mr Tang Hai Liang. He is still active at his sundry shop.

to cater to the increasing number of devotees. This was further extended to appease the spirit of a lady who perished at sea.

A group of people queues to see Miss Wong's father, to have their fortunes read by him. Siow Kian, 33, was born in Ubin and has been living there since. Her house is located next to the Ubin Granite Quarry and her backyard is filled with fruit trees.

She started school life at Bin Kiang School in 1974, cycling to class daily. Some of the lessons took place outdoors and that was especially true when learning about science. Siow Kian also contributed to scientific records. When she was about 19, a villager told her that something had fallen to the floor of the quarry. She grabbed her camera and rushed there on a motorbike. Her photograph of the fallen tapir is important for records in Natural History — without which no one would have ever believed that such a mammal existed in Ubin.

Her sister, Sook Kuan, 26, belongs to the last batch of students from Bin Kiang School. Then, everyone knew everyone else, including schoolmates and not just classmates. She still keeps in touch with many of them. Recess time meant going back home for lunch or hanging out at the jetty. It was not uncommon for pupils not to return for lessons on time. This irked the teachers who had to round up the students. She remembers friends who went to

Left: Ms Wong Siow Kian posing by her *jambu air* tree. The fruit is commonly planted around *kampung* homes and eaten as it is or used as a salad. Visitors to the temple often cannot resist the temptation of plucking the succulent fruits.

Below left: Ms Wong Sook Kuan with her trusty two-wheeler. She is rather proficient in manoeuvring the motorbike — having mastered the skills on the island that would qualify her for motocross racing.

Below left: Encik Latif bin Ahmad posed by a lone Ipil tree (*Intsia bijuga*). The roots of this tree and the adjacent Nipah palms anchor the sandy shore by his house, protecting the breakwaters from eroding the shoreline.

Below right: Mr Seah Ah Bau, 77, poses with the Giant Snakehead or *Toman*. Still as busy, his daily chores fill his whole day. For him, work is pleasurable and sickness is almost unheard of. Part of his work involves keeping track of ripening fruits in his vast pineapple plantation, plucking the fruit before the wild pigs get to them.

the toilet frequently whenever they were bored with their lessons. The teachers also grew more innovative — they invented ghost stories to stop pupils from playing truant.

Islanders had unusual pets and Sook Kuan was no exception. She kept a pig as a pet and that elicited some fond memories whenever she talked about it. She cried for days when her family sold the pig. It had become too big to handle and had been destroying things around the house. It was worse when the family was told that it tasted excellent.

Sook Kuan's childhood memories include seeing crocodiles in the nearby rivers, feasting on the discarded chickens that perished in large numbers during viral epidemics. She shuttled around the island on a motorbike, happy to visit the family's prawn farm near the Ma Chor Temple at OBS Camp 2. She now lives in Bedok and almost every Sunday, her son will insist on returning to Ubin where he can roam free, play with cousins, feed the chicken and ducks and pluck fruits. Shopping malls have no meaning for him.

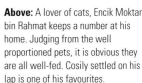

One day at a time

While the younger people have options, there are few left for the older folks of Ubin. A community leader, Encik Latif bin Ahmad, 79, was the great grandson of Ubin pioneer Endut Senin, founder of Kampung Surau. In his younger days, Encik Latif chose to live in Kampong Surau too, but he now lives with his children on the mainland.

Most islanders get by from day to day, moving through their routines of chores that define their lives on Ubin. Some still work, some still farm. All are too strongly attached to their island home to consider leaving.

Independent and carefree, Mr Seah Ah Bau, 77, has been living on the island for more than 20 years. He willingly showed us his vast pineapple plantation. He has to keep track of his ripened fruits so that he can pluck them before the wild boars get to them. His *chiku* tree boasts of fruits larger than usual. He usually sells these fruits to visitors at a temple just after the Jelutong Bridge. A bachelor, his abode is a dilapidated house with a well. For Mr Seah, the lack of electricity is not a problem. The lack of light means more reflective moments and uninterrupted sleep.

Retired and alone, Encik Moktar bin Rahmat thinks he is more than 70 years old — he cannot be certain. He was born in Pulau Tekong but he settled at Kampung Melayu in the 1970s after he was re-trenched when the British Forces left Singapore. Like Encik Sulung, he also worked as a mosquito sprayer.

He was interned by the Japanese during World War II and was sent to New Britain (lying just north-east of New Guinea, the island of New Britain was captured by the Japanese in 1942 and became a part of Papua New Guinea in 1975) to be a construction worker. He lost all his family members during the war. Still a bachelor, he finds comfort in his cats — he keeps more than five of them; to him they are his family. Across his shed, further down the road, at an elevated area lies the site of the former Malay school — no longer recognisable with disused kerosene lamps strewn around.

Above: A lover of cats, Encik Moktar bin Rahmat keeps a number at his home. Judging from the well proportioned pets, it is obvious they are all well-fed. Cosily settled on his lap is one of his favourites.

Left: For Mr Zhong Chun Wang, Pulau Ubin was a place to hide. If he had not left Malaysia to live on Ubin, he could have been forced to become a communist insurgent.

Right: Bronzed by years in the sun, Encik Madon bin Adam, 93, still finds work meaningful. Age has not enfeebled his efforts in thatching the Nipah leaves used for roofing.

Opposite: Mdm Ang Siew Eng weighed the two ducks that she had cornered and caught with a net. In traditional fashion, she handpicked the feathers after scalding the birds. She prefers the ducks to have grown just beyond 90 days before slaughtering them. Strapping the duck between her legs, she deftly tied the duck's feet before weighing it on a *dacing* (a simplified weighing scale). She then held down the feathers before executing the coup de grâce — she deftly slit the duck's neck and removed the windpipe.

Mr Zhong Chun Wang's life was dramatically changed one night in 1951. He fled from his hometown in Batu Pahat, Malaysia, to escape impending enlistment by the much feared communists. He was only 22. Together with his wife, they settled in Pulau Ubin where he had a brother.

Like his brother, he too worked as a rubber tapper. From 1968 to 1990, he worked at the HDB Granite Quarry. He remembered his fellow workers who did not protect themselves from the dust, succumbing to lung infections. He himself is deaf in the left ear, having endured periodic dynamite blasting of the granite. At 71, he and his wife work as caretakers at the Civil Service Club chalets.

Encik Madon bin Adam, 93, worked his nimble fingers aligning the fronds of the Nipah plant so that he could thatch them for use as roofing material. Originally from Pulau Tekong, he has been staying in Ubin for 18 years. The yellow painted plank walls of his home in Kampung Melayu are not easily missed.

For Encik Madon, living on the island means living frugally. A peep into his house only reveals basic necessities. Quiet moments are spent with his wife. They still communicate with each other in soft tones that speak volumes of their affection for each other.

The shopkeepers and eating places expect to see more business when the island is developed. But once developed, most of Ubin's small entrepreneurs will

Above: Cik Latifah bte Taib, picking tapioca leaves for cooking. Her daily requirements are simple and she is in charge of her own time.

ture. What she owns may be swallowed up by future developments. No news might just mean good news.

But whatever news comes from the mainland, life's gentle routines act like a kind of buffer for Cik Latifah binte Taib, 44, a homemaker. She was picking young tapioca leaves for cooking when we interrupted her in her garden. Born in Kampung Melayu, she was educated at the Sekolah Melayu Pulau Ubin (the Malay Primary School of Pulau Ubin) and later at the Changkat Changi Secondary School at Changi. Her present home stands on family land that was recently acquired by the Land Office. She knows that she will have to move out one day, but for now, she is happy and comfortable just being on the island.

The aroma of the *sambal belacan* permeates her cluttered kitchen, lit in evenings by the warm glow of kerosene lamps that hang on long nails along the centre beams of the ceiling. Stirred briskly over the kerosene fire, the red chilli turns a shade of brown. The aroma grows increasingly intoxicating, precipitating torrents of gastric juices. It tickles my nose and makes me sneeze. Tapioca leaves fried with *sambal belacan* is tantalising enough, but boiled with coconut extract and lemon grass, the dish is irresistible.

Time slows down but not enough and we must leave, just as Cik Latifah must too, someday. But for now, life goes on at a walking pace — slow enough for one to stop and smell the *belacan*.

probably be swallowed by bigger businesses. For Mdm Ang Siew Eng, 71, her days in Pulau Ubin too, seemed numbered. She has been staying in Pulau Ubin since 1956. She came from China at the age of nine and settled in Katong before coming over to Ubin to work in the quarry.

She invested some money in a prawn farm but that failed due to pollution from the quarrying works. If she leaves Ubin, she will no longer have the luxury of the space, the fruit orchard, vegetable plot and the poultry farm around her landed property. There will no longer be any live ducks and chicken for her to pluck the feathers from. So for now, she stays, but she might not have a choice about that in the near fu-

Tarzan Boy

Encik Hazali bin Maruf (now about 27) was once known as the "Tarzan of Ubin". He was featured in *The Sunday Times* (7/6/1992) for his uncanny ability to climb trees. His childhood playmates were a group of wild monkeys and he was often up in the trees playing with them instead of with children his own age. Some islanders considered the monkeys pests and Encik Hazali's favourite monkey, which he named Ndi, was shot. He also had less time for his monkey friends after he started attending Bin Kiang School (*The Straits Times*, 1/4/1980). The Long-tailed Macaques are no longer easily sighted now as they have retreated deeper to the secondary forests. Islanders do not know where Hazali bin Maruf lives now or what he does.

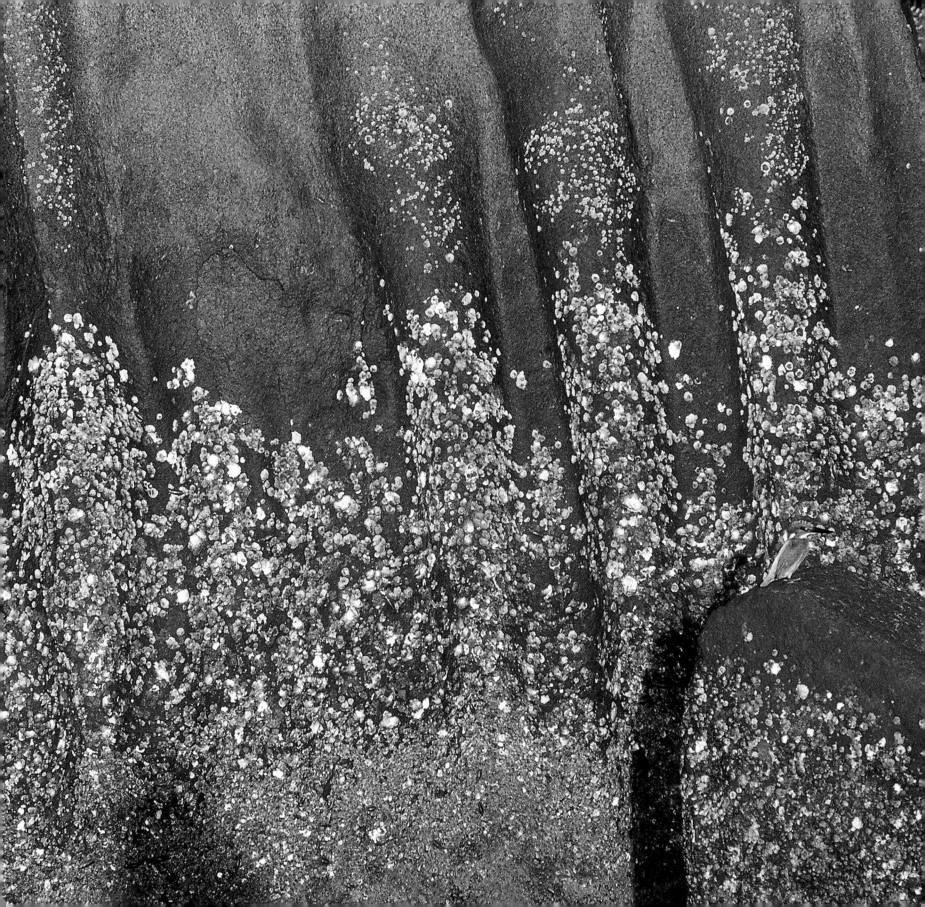

NATURE IN THE BALANCE

The island is a repository for a rich variety of flora and fauna. A total of 179 species of birds have been recorded in Pulau Ubin. This is about 50 per cent of all birds found in Singapore. A total of 382 species of vascular plants have been reported on Pulau Ubin. There are only 25 mammal species.

Records show the island has the only known population of the Long-tongued Nectar Bat (*Macroglossus minimus*) and Leopard Cat (*Felis bengalensis*)[25]. Viable populations of Wild Boars (*Sus scrofa*) exist. The Common Palm Civet (*Paradoxurus hermaphroditus*) has been regularly sighted. The Dugong (*Dugong dugon*) is rarely sighted but has been known to feed on the coastal waters of the island. Ironically, its presence was noted only after a carcass was washed ashore. Other than Pulau Ubin, the rare Oriental Small-clawed Otter (*Aonyx cinerea*) has not been seen anywhere else in Singapore. Tomb bats, fruit bats and flying foxes are also found on Ubin.

Opposite: Barnacles on the rock faces and a Common Kingfisher (*Alcedo atthis*) strategically perched as it scans the waters for vulnerable signs of fish surfacing.

Right: The Pacific Reef Egret (*Egretta sacra*) can be commonly seen on the mudflats of Pulau Ubin feeding on fish, molluscs and crustaceans.

Right: Aerial view of Sungei Besar mangroves. The lush flora is important for wildlife to continue to exist but its importance is often underestimated.

Opposite, bottom right: Beautifully coloured, the Mangrove Pitta (*Pitta megarhyncha*) is a rare find in Pulau Ubin. It hops around the floor of mangrove forests feeding on invertebrates.

The mangroves

Skirting the coasts and lining the rivers of Ubin are several species of mangrove plants. These occupy 16.7 per cent of the total land area of Pulau Ubin. Located in the centre of the island are mangrove forests drained by four main tidal rivers — the Sungei Puaka, Sungei Jelutong, Sungei Besar and Sungei Mamam. The highest concentration, just under 195 hectares, is found around Sungei Besar (in the north) and Sungei Batu Kekek (right of the HDB Granite Quarry).

Rarely seen is the large copper-coloured fruit of the *Xylocarpus granutum* (which is the size of a grapefruit) as it glows in the morning sun. Found in the estuarine waters in the northeast region, this mangrove plant is uncommon. The tree is about 3 to 8 m tall and its flowers are white and fragrant. Just as tall is the *Lumnitzera littorea* that can be seen near the orchid farm. Its bright red flowers are an attractive diversion to the otherwise dull green or grey surroundings. The *Bruguiera gymnorhiza* also has red flowers but not as showy as *L. littorea* and is commonly seen on the southeast coast.

Plants of the mangrove forest are vulnerable to the changing salinity of the surrounding waters and adaptations are necessary for the plants to survive. Some plants excrete excess salt through salt glands (like the *Avicennia* sp.) or through a process of ultra-filtration where only certain ions are selectively absorbed (like the *Bruguiera, Lumnitzera, Rhizophora* or *Sonneratia* spp.). The *Avicennia alba* and *Sonneratia alba* dominate the seaward zone where there is frequent flooding with sea water. More inland are the *Rhizophora* spp. where the arched anchor roots retain the tide-borne mud.

Most mangrove plants have their young plants germinating whilst still attached to the parent plant. Having the advantage of germination maximises the chances of survival in the most demanding of environments.

The root systems of mangrove plants provide not only stability and support, they also have erect roots or pnuematophores (breathing roots) to adapt to the poorly oxygenated soils. These pneumatophores come in several forms: pencil-like in *Avicennia* and *Sonneratia* spp., prop and stilt roots in *Rhizophora* spp., kneed roots in *Bruguiera* and *Lumnitzera* and plank roots in *Xylocarpus granatum*.

The mangrove forest serves as nursery grounds for young fish and prawns. Sheltered and with less turbulent tides, fish fry develop and grow before

Left and top: The bright red sepals and the fruiting branch of the rare mangrove plant, *Bruguiera gymnorhiza*. Its trunk makes good firewood and charcoal.

Above, centre: *Sonneratia alba* — these mangrove plants are found just at the jetty. Its persimmon-like fruits and leaves can be eaten. Its flowers are pollinated by bats.

Above: A living fossil. Prehistoric yet still surviving well is the Horseshoe Crab (*Carcinoscorpius rotundicauda*). Research work on this animal revealed the importance of its blood in detecting bacterial contamination, especially in the food industry.

Right: Common in mangrove areas, the Archer Fish (*Toxotes jaculatrix*) is able to purse its lips and eject a stream of water to dislodge insects on branches drooping low over water or exposed arched roots of mangrove plants through its pursed mouth. As it is a surface feeder, it can be easily seen at the waters of the Changi and Ubin jetty.

Opposite: A Pulai tree (*Alstonia angustiloba*), the tallest tree on the island. It is believed to be about 80 to 100 years old.

A Horseshoe Crab lies on its back, apparently overturned. As it struggles, its tail pierces deeper into the sand to create an arch by which it can flip over. It can only attempt to flip a few more times before it will start to die under the scorching sun.

Fresh mounds of Mud Lobsters (*Thalassina anomala*) line the paths of mangrove forests and fish farms. It is said they are difficult to see for they only appear at night. Since they live in an extensive network of burrows, they are almost impossible to catch.

Some of the last of the Nipah palm (*Nypa fruticans*) mangroves in Singapore is found on Pulau Ubin. The main patch is located at Kampung Melayu and scattered patches are also found at Kampung Surau and near the RDC (or Gammon) quarry. Bright golden inflorescence give an indication where the cluster of fruits will be attached. The short trees have leaves like coconut trees; some scattered fronds of brown fruits lie waiting to be harvested. The fruits appear as a large clump but getting to them in the muddy terrain is no

maturing in deeper waters. The mangroves' existence is thus vital to the continued supply of diverse fishes in the sea. Mangroves also help to reclaim land where silt and organic matter are retained around the complex root systems. Housing developments on the island will almost surely destroy the last of the rare mangrove plants.

Fiddler crabs adorn the shore, playing a game of hide-and-seek. Moving cautiously and not far from the security of their burrows, they sieve the fine silt for food. The male Fiddler Crab (*Uca* spp.) waves its asymmetrical claws like a one-armed bandit, perhaps displaying a message to a potential mate.

Mudskippers (F. Gobiidae), camouflaged against the mud, jump into the safety of water when disturbed. The alternating movements of their pectoral fins create a wiggle; less noticeable when it moves with greater urgency.

easy matter. Often too hard and too ripe, the fruits are wonderful when preserved and served as dessert (*atap chee*). The mature leafs are used for thatching roofs.

Beach or coastal plants include the Sea Hibiscus (*Hibiscus tiliaceus*) and the Sea Lettuce (*Scaevola taccada*). Rarely seen, the Screwpine (*Pandanus odoratissimus*) plant is found on the southeastern part of Ubin among the mangrove forest where boats are usually repaired. It has bright orange fruits and its large leaves can be used for mats and baskets.

The secondary forest

The secondary forest is important for the diverse bird and mammal species found on the island. It makes up 50.6 per cent of the land area, which includes the abandoned rubber plantations, farms and fruit orchards. In the west, the hills of Bukit Tajam (56 m) and Bukit Tinggi (58 m) and its surroundings secondary forests form a major part of the land area of the Outward Bound Singapore and much of the undisturbed secondary forests. Other good stands of secondary forest lie towards the east at Kampung Melayu, Tanjung Chek Jawa and the Sam Heng Estate.

One of the largest trees on the island is the Pulai tree (*Alstonia angustiloba*), which is estimated to be about more than 80 years old. Its massive plank buttress partly surrounds a solitary pair of Muslim tombstones which probably is of the same age.

Right: The brown slime on the stem of the Stinkhorn fungus (*Phallus* sp.) gives off an unpleasant odour which is meant to attract flies. It also contains spores. The encounter is unusual at the highest point in Pulau Ubin. Likely to be erect when fresh, it deteriorates rapidly; auto-digesting within a few hours.

Far right: Inflorescence of Nipah palm (*Nypa fruticans*). Mature fruits are harvested where the young seeds are extracted and mixed with syrup and made to an edible desert called "atap chee". Sap from the inflorescence stalk can be used to make toddy (a potent alcoholic drink), vinegar and sugar. Mature leaves can be used for thatching material whilst the young leaves, for cigarette wrappers.

The tree has a magnificent crown that can be seen from afar. Also known as a "pagoda tree", the multi-tiered profile of the tree is obvious. Beyond this tree towards the east, the drooping branches of the *Penaga Laut* (*Calophyllum inophyllum*) lie over the light brown rocks and waves.

The exuberant orange flowers usually catch one's eye while one cycles through the rubber (*Hevea brasiliensis*) plantation. The blooms of wild Ixoras (*Ixora congesta*) are like bouquets of food for the many sunbirds whose fine curved beaks are just right for the extraction of nectar. Large yellow-brown leaves of rubber trees are translucent against the skylight and their vein patterns clearly defined if one cares to look at them. The occasional popping sounds are due to the splitting of the rubber tree fruit discharging its seeds. Wild boars help to control the spread of rubber trees by feeding on these seeds.

Uncommon, but by the edge of the HDB Granite Quarry, is a healthy stand of Slender Pitchers (*Nepenthes gracilis*) in rather nutrient-poor soils. This pitcher and the Narrow-Lidded Pitcher (*N. ampullaria*) are found near the reservoir of Outward Bound Singapore. An occasional cluster of flowers of a climber, *Hoya* sp., lies delicately overhead in tree branches. Large globular orange figs (*Ficus* sp.) are also found high up in trees, noticed only when scraps of the fruits are found on the floor when mammals and birds feed on them. The large deep green leaves of wild yams (*Dioscorea* sp.) are conspicuous on some of the trails.

Although not a true rhododendron, the Singapore Rhododendron (*Melastoma malabathricum*) is scattered across the island. It has attractive pink or light purple flowers and its berries often attract birds. Birds also feed on the red fruits of the *Simpoh Air* (*Dillenia suffruiticosa*) and it is not usual for its fruits to stay attached for long periods on the dehisced sepals. Its large leaves were once used to wrap food. Along the paths, it is not uncommon to come across many wild flowers introduced from South America like the Prickly Lantana (*Lantana camara*), Common Snakeweed (*Stachytarpheta indica*) and Water Lemon (*Passiflora foetida*). The yellow fruit of the Water Lemon is encased by a basket of moss-like leaves.

A total of 29.6 per cent of the vascular plants found in Ubin are the result of a high degree of human intervention (introduced species 19.4 per cent and cultivated species 10.2 per cent).

Left: Fruit of *Xylocarpus granatum*. The mangrove plant is rare on the island. Its trunk is used in boat-building and furniture wood and its bark for tanning.

Below: *Uvaria hirsuta* — one of the rare plants found on the island.

Bottom left: The berry-like orange/scarlet fruits of Tembusu (*Fagraea fragrans*) are sought after by birds and bats. Its flowers are very fragrant (hence its scientific name) and attract moths that pollinate them. Chopping boards were made from its trunks.

Coconut palms (*Cocos nucifera*) are common in Ubin and its existence has also given rise to the "web-of-life" on the island. The larvae of the Palm King butterfly (*Amathusia phidippus*) and the adult Rhinoceros beetle (*Oryctes rhinoceros*) feed on the young developing palms. These insects are, in turn, eaten by the many birds on the island. The Rhinoceros beetles bores into young leaf base of palm leaves of coconut trees making serrated cuts that one sees in the adult leaves. The damaged growing plant results in loss of the coconut yield. Eggs are laid in rotting vegetation and hence there is more infestation due to infrequent clearing of the unwanted vegetation. Termite mounds and Pigeon Orchids (*Dendrobium crumenatum*) are also attached to the tree trunks. Bats roost under the leaves during the day and some birds nest in holes made in trunks of dead coconut trees.

Opposite, centre: Found in the forests surrounding the reservoir of the OBS, the Narrow-Lidded Pitcher (*Nepenthes ampullaria*) is more commonly found on the ground; often in a rosette-like cluster.

Opposite, bottom: Originating from South America, the Water Lemon or Passion Fruit (*Passiflora foetida*) is a climber with scented violet and white flowers. The Long-tailed Macaques feed on the large egg-shaped fruits.

The birds

The Hill Myna's (*Gracula religiosa*) calls are loud strident notes: "Tiong, tiong!" This bird is often trapped and reared as a pet due to its ability in mimicking sounds. Caged ones are openly displayed in some homes. The Malay names for birds are often onomatopoeic. Like *Burung Tiong* for the Hill Myna. Or like the monotonous "boot, boot" from the Greater Coucal (*Centropus sinensis*) or *Burung But But*. Because of its black and brown plumage, it is also called a Crow Pheasant and when sighted, scrambles clumsily amongst the branches. Hidden in the foliage, the Straw-headed Bulbul (*Pycnonotus zeylanicus*) sings in distinctive tunes. Endangered worldwide, the Bulbul needs the mangrove forest to survive.

A sunbird feasts on an overripe rambutan, the skin already a deep darkish red and the translucent fruit barely visible. The Copper-throated Sunbirds (*Nectarinia calcostetha*) usually nest in mangrove forests. Here by the mangrove swamps, they nest at an orchid farm using the firm stalks of the orchid plants to suspend their nest. Low nests made of dried grass and leaves are delicately suspended on small branches by the Olive-backed Sunbirds (*Nectarinia jugularis*). Once noticed, these nests and their eggs easily become collector's items. It is also always a joy to listen to the melodious calls of the Oriental Magpie Robin (*Copsychus saularis*); something we can do without having to cage them. On the mainland, it was once nearly extinct; hopefully its numbers in Ubin will reach healthy levels.

Even louder are the calls from the Collared King-

Above: A winter visitor, the Blue-tailed Bee-eater (*Merops phillippinus*) can be roosting in mangroves. It can be seen in large numbers catching insects on the wing; its familiar tail-feathers is distinct as it glides.

Above right: Rare, the Straw-headed Bulbul (*Pycnonotus zeylanicus*) is found in small numbers on Ubin. Its habitats include the woodlands, river banks and mangrove forests. Its bubbly and melodious calls are characteristic. One has a good chance of hearing its calls on the island.

Right: The Hill Myna (*Gracula religiosa*) is a popular cage bird as it is able to mimic human speech and other bird-calls. Uncommon but still present in Ubin, it is easily mistaken for the Common Myna except for its larger size, loud calls and yellow flaps on its face and nape.

Above: Common in coastal mangroves, the Olive-backed Sunbird (*Nectarinia jugularis*) is not choosy where it builds its nest. Often on low branches, small trees in gardens and parks, the nest resembles a small woven pouch. Males have the characteristic metallic blue throat.

Left and overleaf, top left: A mangrove bird, the Copper-throated Sunbird's (*Nectarinia calcostetha*) iridescent dark copper throat and purple breast are attractive. Stalks from the cultivated orchids serve as scaffoldings for its nest.

Right: The Large-tailed Nightjar (*Caprimulgus macrurus*) is a master of camouflage. On the ground its colouration (eggs, chicks and adults) often deceives the keen-sighted. Its monotonous loud "tok-tok" calls at night are its only giveaway.

Bottom inset: The Rufous-tailed Tailorbird (*Orthotomus sericeus*), like most tailorbirds does not sit still and is often difficult to photograph. It belongs to the Warbler family — small insectivorous birds with narrow pointed bills. Commonly seen at the mangrove forests and coastal shrubs, the bird makes nests from leaves that are stitched together using spider's webs.

fisher (*Halcyon chloris*). It is not easy to distinguish the subtly different calls of the many birds in Ubin. But bird-watchers will tell you that it is the calls that lead one to the birds. The brilliant blue wings of the White-throated Kingfisher (*Halcyon smyrnensis*) are dazzling. But most impressive is an even larger kingfisher, the Stork-billed Kingfisher (*Pelargopsis capensis*).

The Brahminy Kite (*Haliastur indus*) encircles the quarry lake, gliding in search of prey. It soars and descends, taking advantage of the thermals and winds, its bright brown plumage spotlighted by the glow of the setting sun.

The nest of the White-bellied Fish-eagle (*Haliaeetus leucogaster*) is like a huge cauldron of twigs. Usually constructed on a tall dead tree, its choice of residence often sticks out like a sore thumb. Mated

Left: Reddish-brown and less distinctive than the other woodpeckers, the Rufous Woodpecker (*Celeus brachyurus*) is now not commonly seen. It consumes large amounts of ants and termites; often raiding their nests but consuming a little from each nest each day. It practises a sustainable form of harvesting, ensuring its food supply never runs out — something we humans rarely practise.

Bottom left: More commonly seen than heard, the Indian Cuckoo's (*Cuculus micropterus*) habitat is the secondary forests of Pulau Ubin.

Bottom right: The White-throated Kingfisher (*Halcyon smyrnensis*) often sits on a low branch — ready to pounce on small creatures. It flashes its brilliant blue wing feathers as it flies.

Right: For a kingfisher, the Stork-billed Kingfisher (*Pelargopsis capensis*) is relatively large. It is one of the most brilliantly coloured and has a massive red bill. It usually sits on branches overlooking water, diving to catch fish.

Below: The Collared Kingfisher (*Halcyon chloris*) advertises its presence with its loud calls. The bird feeds on insects, small crabs, worms and small reptiles. It nests in holes along embankments of rivers or cavities in mangrove trees.

pairs take turns to incubate the eggs. They often land at the adjacent trees before approaching the nests; a safeguard against the obvious. Its chick is coloured completely brown and amidst the branches and twigs of the nest, it will be less obvious to aerial predators. This is important when both parents are away for longer periods looking for more food to feed the ravenous appetites of its young.

A Black-headed Munia (*Lonchura malacca*) is feeding on some grass seeds; its rich plumage makes it one of the more attractive Munias. More common are the Scaly-breasted Munias (*Lonchura punctulata*). The stalk of grass seeds suddenly collapses from the

weight of these Munias as they land on them. Their strong beaks are able to crush the seed coverings.

A smaller version of the domesticated chicken, the male Red Junglefowl (*Gallus gallus*) has brilliantly coloured feathers, a white cheek patch and grey legs. Not the most consummate of fliers, this fowl often makes short distance flights. Frequently followed by the female and its brood of chicks, the fowl is vulnerable to poachers. There was an occasion when a nature lover had to negotiate with a poacher to purchase three fowls that were destined for the dinner table. The transaction took place in the confines of an out-going boat. Fortunately, the three fowls were returned to Ubin; but at a price.

Under the Albizia trees (*Paraserienthes falcataria*) beside the Ho Man Choo Granite Quarry, five Southern Pied Hornbills (*Anthracoceros albirostris*) fly in formation and glide to the nearby branches. It seems unreal that hornbills should be found in Singapore. As many as nine have been sighted on the island. It is not known how long the forests of Ubin can sustain these huge birds. Even the Red-breasted Parakeets (*Psittacula alexandri*) are finding the island's habitats an important breeding site.

The poles at the *kelong* are a perfect vantage point for the Grey Heron (*Ardea cinerea*). The man-made fish ponds are often visited by migrant waders like the Common Greenshank (*Tringa nebularia*), Common Redshank (*Tringa totanus*), Plovers (*Pluvialis squatarola* and *Pluvialis fulva*; *Charadrius dubius* and *Charadrius mongolus*) and Egrets (*Egretta* spp.).

The bunds of these ponds are also roosting sites during high tide. Like the waders, that are not easily spotted, viewing the Yellow Bittern (*Ixobrychus sinensis*) needs some form of camouflage and patience. A small pond surrounded by long grass is the only natural freshwater pond on the island. A White-breasted Waterhen (*Amaurornis phoenicurus*) moved gingerly by the water edge, furtively glancing at approaching visitors.

Above: Colourful and noisy, the pink breast is diagnostic for the Red-breasted Parakeet (*Psittacula alexandri*). It travels in groups and on occasions has been seen mingling with the Long-tailed Parakeets. The parakeet is favoured by fortune-tellers as the bird is quite adept at picking out cards.

Left: The strong conical beak of the Black-headed Munia (*Lonchura malacca*) is ideal for cracking grass seeds. It normally travels in flocks and is common in grasslands.

Below: The Yellow Bittern (*Ixobrychus sinensis*) is capable of "freezing" and looking skywards among the reeds where it lays indistinguishable from its surroundings. The brown colouration and body streaks aid the camouflage.

Bottom: The Little Heron (*Butorides striatus*) nests in mangroves areas where it spends most of its time crouching on mudflats looking for prey.

Other birds that visitors can easily spot are the Pink-necked Green Pigeons (*Treron vernans*), Yellow-vented Bulbuls (*Pycnontus goiavier*), Asian Glossy Starlings (*Aplonis panayensis*), Common Iora (*Aegithina tiphia*) and Peaceful Doves (*Geopelia striata*). The Collared-scops Owl (*Otus bakkamoena*) and Spotted Wood Owl (*Strix seloputo*) are commonly heard at night.

Opposite, right: The Little Egret (*Egretta garzetta*) is identified by its conspicuous yellow feet and pair of breeding plumes on the rear of its crown.

Above: A small and shy bird, the Collared scops-Owl's (*Otus bakkamoena*) mournful call sometimes resembles that of a cat. It feeds on invertebrates like grasshoppers and beetles and is also known to eat small vertebrates. It sits on a low perch, pouncing on prey moving on the ground. This Owl was netted during a night survey and was tagged and released.

Left: Rarely seen during the day, the Spotted Wood Owl (*Strix seloputo*) was roosting on low branches of a tree near the mangrove forest.

Far left: The bright yellow iris of the Buffy Fish Owl (*Ketupa ketupu*) is prominent as the torchlight catches its eyes. Rather large in size, the owl's yellow brown plumage makes it one of the most attractive owls. It feeds on fish, frogs and other small vertebrates. When noticed during the day, it is known to compress its plumage to appear like a piece of wood. A pair had been spotted nesting near the orchid farm.

Above: Cicada shell and emerging cicada. Almost like the real thing — in intricate details. Nature is amazing, for like this shell it is inconceivable how it really happened the way it did; like a programmed chip. Who is this programmer, anyway?

Below left: Great Egg-fly (*Hypolimnas bolina*).

Below right: Common Tiger (*Danaus genutia*). The forests and wooded areas are the last resorts for our butterflies.

Insects

Night surveys can be exciting on Pulau Ubin. On a tree just by Noordin Beach, an Atlas Moth (*Attacus atlas*), fresh from its transformation from the pupa, displayed its delicate wings as it dried under the moonlight. Just a short distance away, a pale-green caterpillar of the same moth which was feeding on the leaves, froze as the branch was accidentally touched. The cicada pupa too found the weather to be auspicious for it to crawl out of the earth and start transforming into an adult.

Two Gray's Malayan Stick Insects (*Lonchodes brevipes*) were feeding on the edges of young leaves. One suddenly just fell flat and played dead, looking like a fallen branch. After 10 minutes it seemed to tire of its pranks and when the danger seemed to have passed, it began functioning again. Such is the wonder of nature.

Butterflies found on the island include the Black-veined Albatross (*Appias libythea*), Painted Jezebel (*Delia hyparete*) and the Horsfield's Baron (*Tanaecia iapis*).

The pretty Common Tiger (*Danaus genutia*) flaunts its stripes as it stops atop the capitulum of the wildflowers. The Great Mormon (*Papilio memnon*) darts around the wild Ixoras looking for nectar.

Spiders often lie in wait smack in the centre of their delicate web. Vibrations from the web will precipitate an instant scramble; like an angler whose bait that has just been taken. An insect is entangled in the web and the larger female spider will reach the prey first. The venom works fast. Satisfied with a minor

Above: The Dark Glassy Tiger (*Parantica agleoides*) mimics the poisonous Blue Glassy Tiger in vein patterns. Hence it is spared from predation.

Left: Discovered during a night survey, the Atlas Moth (*Attacus atlas*) with its outstretched wings appears to be drying its wings. One of the largest moths in the world, its dull green caterpillar is just as large (below right).

Below left: Almost impossible to detect during the day, the Gray's Malayan Stick Insect (*Lonchodes brevipes*) has impeccable camouflage. Reddish brown and scrawny, it is indistinguishable from the twig it rests on. It is most vulnerable when it feeds at night. At that time however, nocturnal predators must have excellent vision. When threatened, it falls on its side to appear like a fallen twig and stays motionless until the danger is over.

feast, it might probably let its mate have the next meal.

The web from the Golden-web Spider (*Nephila maculata*) glitters with a tinge of gold (hence the name) when struck by the rays of sunlight. Another species of the same size but with deep brown legs and a black body is also common.

An Atlas Moth dangles from what looks like strands of spider webs. It tries frantically to escape by fluttering its wings; its huge size generates much force but it is in vain. The webs hold. Exhausted, it sways with the breeze as it awaits its untimely demise.

Opposite, left to right: The vivid colours of the Malay Lacewing (*Cethosia hypsea*); Fivebar Swordtail (*Pathysa antiphates*); and Palm King (*Amathusia phidippus*).

Opposite, bottom: While the birds feast on the figs during the day, this cricket (F. Orthoptera) took the opportunity during the night. That way, the nocturnal insect is not preyed upon by the birds.

Below: The Malabar Spider (*Nephilengys malabarensis*) is found in secondary forest and mangrove swamps. It commonly builds webs near surfaces of tree trunks. Seen here is a female (which is five times the size of the male) drawing fluids from a trapped grasshopper.

Left: Red Tent Spider (*Cyrthophora unicolor*). The web of this spider is an intricate three-dimensional structure. The spider hides in a curled leaf suspended in the centre of the web.

Far left: Golden Web Spider (*Nephila maculata*). The male is puny compared to the much larger female. Mating can be fatal for the male if it does not send proper signals to the female, which might eat the male.

Above: A centipede (*Scolopendra subspinipes*).

Below: A menacing Black Scorpion (*Heterometrus longimanus*) — its hairy, glistening tail poised to strike.

Above right: The Green Crested Lizard's (*Bronchocela cristatella*) colour effectively camouflages it from prey and predators.

Reptiles

Changeable lizards (*Calotes versicolor*) flaunting their dark necks to potential mates can be spotted under direct sunlight. The coconut tree trunks are perfect for their daily "sun-tan".

Less obvious are the slimmer Flying Lizards (*Draco volans*); their dull colours camouflage them well. Their prelude to mating is more elaborate with yellow, flashing neck flaps. They glide effortlessly using outstretched skin membranes.

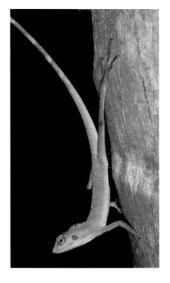

Opposite, top right: Mating behaviour of Flying Lizard (*Draco volans*). Triangular throat flags flap repeatedly to attract the mate's attention.

Opposite, bottom right: Less than half the length of the Water Monitor (*Varanus salvator*), the Clouded Monitor (*Varanus nebulosus*) lives in forested areas. Here, it finds refuge in a damaged water pipe.

Above: Arboreal and diurnal, the Paradise Tree Snake (*Chrysopelea paradisi*) is able to climb tree trunks with ease due to the keeled belly scales. It is known to launch itself from great heights by flattening and drawing in its ventral surface to trap a cushion of air to act like a parachute.

Above left: A rare Shore Pit Viper (*Trimeresurus purpureomaculatus*). Venomous and nocturnal, this viper is a first record for Pulau Ubin. It is often coiled up in mangrove trees. Generally purplish brown, its colour varies.

Green-crested Lizards (*Bronchocela cristatella*) hide in the undergrowth aided by their deep green colour whilst Water Monitors (*Varanus salvator*) frequent the mudflats of the mangroves and prawn farms looking for crabs, small animals and will have a go at the domesticated chicken. Frequently flashing its forked tongue, the Water Monitor is able to detect carrion. Sensory organs are located in its tongue. Although it appears a little sluggish on land, it is still able to run well when necessary. It is also able to swim.

Mammals

Park officers have been dismantling wild boar traps set up on the island. Some families of wild boars have been spotted during the day but it is more likely they move around at night when they are less noticed.

A Leopard Cat trapping was reported once.[26] Diminutive and attractive, this mammal has not been seen in Singapore for years. It was later released after persuasion from members of the Nature Society.

It was in 1991 when a wild elephant found it necessary to migrate to the island but unfortunately the island was too civilised to accept the animal. It had to be tranquillised by a dart from a rifle[27] and later coaxed by two trained female elephants to return to Johor[28]. This was the first time such a large mammal had been found on Ubin. In 1990, three elephants were spotted in Pulau Tekong.

Some residents reported that they had come

Opposite, left: Found in Pulau Ubin, the Long-tongued Nectar Bat (*Macroglossus minimus*) is a rare record.

Opposite, right: Wild boar (*Sus scrofa*). Troops of wild boars are common on the island. Thick vegetation facilitates its movements undetected. Young boars have dark horizontal stripes over brown bodies. Its colouration provides effective cover when it rests on the ground. Encouraged by increasing demand for wild boar meat at the restaurants, residents build cages to trap the mammal. Regular patrols by NParks' staff help combat poaching. Here, a cage is being dismantled by NParks' staff (bottom left).

Left: Once thought to be extinct in Singapore, the Leopard Cat (*Felis bengalensis*) still wanders in the wilderness of the Ubin island. Perhaps it is the last one ever reported.

Bottom right: A trapped Common Palm Civet (*Paradoxurus hermaphroditus*). Trapping continues to decimate the populations of birds and mammals on the island.

Above: A dead Dugong. It is uncertain how many are left, but what is certain is that there are not many around. Before it becomes extinct, perhaps a sanctuary could be built so that its continuity is ensured.

Below: Asian Elephant (*Elephas maximus*) — a rare visitor.

across tapirs, porcupines and even a tiger in the past.[29] When a resident reported having seen a tiger, the news created such a flurry of activity that the poor animal probably had to retreat to where it came from. It is hard to tell what else Ubin can offer. But we can be certain that these larger animals can survive only if their habitats are left undisturbed.

Off the island, the Dugong (*Dugong dugon*) has been reported to survive on marine vegetation. A dead Dugong was found near the Ubin Jetty, straddled between the granite boulders of the island.[30] Also known as a Sea Cow, this mammal grazes on sea grasses. It was also reported that a decomposed carcass of the mammal was found near the waters off Pulau Ubin.[31] Yet another decomposing adult was washed ashore near the Changi Cargo Complex.[32]

This large gentle mammal is easily injured as it moves too slowly away from high-speed propellers; if not, the pollution of the surrounding seawater will exterminate the small population of Dugongs. Proposed reclamation works on Ubin and Tekong will surely spell doom for the mammal here.[33] There is a possibility that more may exist. Many hope. But if there are no measures to help them breed, we can just keep on hoping in vain.

Development

Under the Concept Plan for Year X (when the population of Singapore reaches four million), some housing and light industry would be developed on Pulau Ubin and Pulau Tekong.[34] The Urban Redevelopment Authority (URA) intended to accommodate 60,000 people on the island in the future[35] when the population target was reached. That would mean land reclamation, destruction of secondary forests and mangroves. The fate of Ubin thus rests on our population growth! The population was supposed to pass the four million mark after 2010[36] and road and rail networks from the mainland would be extended to Ubin after 2030.

But the population size approached the four million mark by 1999, a decade ahead of schedule.[37] A suggestion by Mr Quek Kwang Ser[38] to relocate the

Sungei Tengah Agro-tech Park to Pulau Ubin and thus free the vast areas in Sungei Tengah for residential housing could perhaps be a viable alternative.

Granite mining destroyed the vast natural expanse and fortunately that has all stopped. Land clearing for developments further diminished the forested and mangrove areas that the wildlife of Ubin depends on.

A resort with facilities for water sports like jet-skiing and scuba diving, and a man-made lagoon has opened.[39] Some are concerned that developments on the island may be so profit-driven that the resort haven may be a case of paradise lost.[40]

Other damage has come from the illegal excavation of three plots of land in the north, totalling 16 hectares.[41] The destruction of the natural habitat threatened the nesting grounds of birds and also affected the marine life.

Pollution by visitors mars the beauty of the island. Poaching of wildlife will further limit the genetic pool for further propagation of the already endangered wildlife. Litter is escalating on trails and beaches. Educating the visitors and people of Ubin not to litter and to take care of the environment is a necessary part of conserving the wildlife of Ubin.

But once the island is developed for housing, the unique flora and fauna we call our very own is doomed to perish.

Above: Quarrying works such as this have resulted in the destruction of Ubin's natural terrain. Fortunately such activities are a thing of the past.

Left: The Spotted-neck Dove (*Streptopelia chinensis*) is a ground-feeding bird, found in open country, secondary forests and villages. It feeds on grass seeds. Its Malay name "Tekukur" is based on the sound it makes. Here the Spotted Dove is used as a decoy. Note the tiny rings of wire that would tighten once the other bird's feet are tangled in it.

Below: Pangolin (*Manis javanica*). A rare sighting on the island, this anteater was photographed in 1993.

Right: Turning one's back on the comforts of modern living to learn the art of simple living.

In his search for answers, Man will reflect on questions about self. In his search for understanding of the wilderness, he is comforted by the balance of nature. In his search for meaning, he is overwhelmed by the powers he is bestowed with. And it is within our powers to save the environment.

The Nature Society of Singapore (NSS) recommended the setting up of a Conservation Council in Ubin to evaluate development projects on the island. The Council would study the feasibility of a wildlife sanctuary in the west, extending to the mangrove areas. A Nature-cum-Cultural Park in the central zone could be established, with the creation of special interest areas like the diminishing Nipah swamps. More details can be found in the NSS's conservation proposal in 1992. A Straits Times reader, Geh Min wrote: "It requires far more planning and foresight for a country to conserve its natural heritage for posterity."[42]

Some may argue that a few plants, birds and mammals should not dictate how we live our lives. But how we live our lives has a direct effect on how the environment is sustained. And the more the environment is sustained, the more enriched our lives will be. The balance of nature — surely we must recognise that it is tilted unfavourably towards our growing population. In increasingly urbanised Singapore, where else can one appreciate the uniqueness of a rural retreat like Pulau Ubin?

The balance of nature

The nature lover will marvel at the simplicities as well as complexities of life. The existence of life on earth is much more profound if one thinks hard enough.

Reflections on Nature in Pulau Ubin, by Subaraj Rajathurai, Nature Guide

Introduction

Little was known about Ubin's wildlife in the 19th and early 20th century. The original rainforest in Pulau Ubin and neighbouring Pulau Tekong were removed around the 1950s and early 60s. Entire hills were blasted off in Ubin together with the rainforest when the island was quarried for granite unlike at the Bukit Timah Nature Reserve where only the fringe was disturbed.

The Diard's Trogon (a forest bird) previously found in Ubin, is now extinct (a specimen was collected on 25 February 1921 and is preserved at the Zoological Reference Collection, NUS). Tapirs are also a historical memory. Nocturnal surveys conducted in 1993 by members of the NSS revealed a diversity of mammals. More surveys were also conducted, this time by the National Parks Board in 1999 and are still continuing.

Vertebrate sightings

The largest bat in the world, the Malayan Flying Fox, visits the island regularly, helping to pollinate durian and other local fruits. The island also supports a healthy population of Common Palm Civets. A villager reported a number of sightings of Leopard Cats on the island. A visitor chanced upon an adult and baby Porcupine foraging near Noordin in 1994. Wild Pigs re-colonised the island in the mid-1980s and over 300 are estimated to be on the island. The waters around still contain the internationally endangered Dugong and the locally threatened Finless Porpoise. There were claims of Cream-coloured Giant Squirrel, Three-striped Palm Civet and even a *Seladang* (Wild Buffalo) on Pulau Ubin. More work is needed to check out these claims.

Pulau Ubin supports the largest population of Red Junglefowl (which probably colonised the island in recent times) and the Straw-headed Bulbul (an internationally vulnerable species) in Singapore. Mangrove dependent species recorded here are the Plaintive Cuckoo and the White-chested Babbler. Another mangrove dependent that is common in Ubin is the Copper-throated Sunbird. Pulau Ubin is also an important refuge for the Oriental Magpie Robin, Rusty-breasted

Cuckoos, Hill Mynas and Laced and Common Flameback Woodpeckers. Visitors to Ubin include Cinnamon-headed and Little Green Pigeons, Green Imperial Pigeon, Crested Serpent Eagle and a Christmas Frigatebird.

Other vertebrates of interest on Ubin include the Banded Krait, a snake rediscovered in 1998. Three other snakes, the Twin-barred Tree Snake, Dog-toothed Cat Snake and Keel-bellied Whip Snake — all forest dependents — somehow survived the loss of habitat. Another forest dependent, the Clouded Monitor, was also found in 1998. There were four records of Estuarine Crocodiles in Ubin.

Exciting encounters

A few years ago, I encountered two Oriental Small-clawed Otters crossing a bund near Kampung Noordin. Before that I had not known they even existed on Ubin. My first encounter with Wild Pigs was also at Kampung Noordin when a large female casually strolled past me in the

Right: Extremely rare in Pulau Ubin, the Cinnamon-headed Green Pigeon (*Treron fulvicollis*) prefers mangrove forests.

mid-1980s. Most satisfying for me was securing the release of a trapped Leopard Cat, back to the wild. The rediscovery of this species after nearly three decades was truly remarkable.

A Long-tongued Nectar Bat was netted during a NSS survey, a first record locally since 1923. Checking road-kills also produced some interesting discoveries. I have collected two Diard's Blind Snakes and a Keel-bellied Whip Snake — both are scarce in Singapore and these were deposited at the Zoological Reference Collection at the NUS.

A more recent new discovery was the sighting of a Northern Hobby which flew low over the village ponds during March 1997 — a first migrant raptor in Singapore. Other migrants include a female Great Frigatebird, Schrenck's Bittern, Siberian Blue Robin and three Swinhoe's Storm Petrels, all seen off the eastern coast of the island.

Proximity with Malaysia also facilitated bird encounters. I first saw the Oriental Pied Hornbill near Asam in March 1991 together with a group of friends. The encounter was so exciting that one of them fell off the bicycle! The hornbill subsequently took up residence in Ubin. Recent colonists from either Malaysia, Tekong, mainland Singapore or elsewhere include the Spotted Wood Owl, Savanna Nightjar, Great-billed Heron and White-rumped Shamas (mid-1980s). I consider myself lucky to report two records of the Black-headed Bulbul on the island.

I discovered a rare Buffy Fish Owl roosting in a rubber estate on the eastern side of the island in March 1988. Now at least four pairs are known to exist in Ubin. On the mainland only one or two pairs are known from Lower Peirce, MacRitchie and Sungei Buloh — making Ubin an important site for the survival of this owl. I also found a Mangrove Pitta at Sungei Besar and to date at least, three birds are confirmed for that area. Rare residents also include the White-rumped Munia and White-chested Babbler. A pair of Black-naped Terns were found nesting on a rock on the northern coast whilst on a boat trip with David Bellamy.

Tourist feedback and thoughts on the future

As a professional natural history and bird guide, I have the opportunity to show Pulau Ubin to many visitors from around the world. Nearly all agree on one thing: Ubin is a superb place and should be preserved for its rich natural, historical and cultural aspects. When they visit Ubin they immediately pronounce that this is exactly what they came to see: the real *kampung*, fruit orchards, rubber estates, prawn ponds and *kelong*. They are also amazed at the birdlife.

Pulau Ubin is best described as a "living museum of old Singapore". For the older generation, it is like coming home, for many grew up in *kampung* while it is a eye-opener for the younger generation as these sights have all disappeared from the mainland. Some tourists are not

Left: Woodlands, secondary growth and plantations are habitats of the Rusty-breasted Cuckoo (*Cacomantis sepulcralis*).

Bottom left: Tree holes are popular nesting sites for the Laced Woodpecker (*Picus vittatus*). The olive plumage and red crown of the male are unmistakable; the female has a black crown. The Laced Woodpecker is commonly seen feeding on insects obtained from tree trunks.

particularly interested in man-made attractions as much can be seen in their own countries. They would rather seek out the undeveloped, natural attractions and once Ubin is developed, they would rather spend their money in neighbouring countries.

Pulau Ubin is already extremely popular for a variety of reasons. These include varied adventure opportunities, nature appreciation and its contagious relaxed atmosphere. The way of life on the island is slowly dying a natural death, helped by the resettlement plan for the villagers. While some villagers survive by managing bicycle rental shops, driving taxis or plying bum-boats to and from Changi, more needs to be done to help them. To experience the flavour of Ubin, perhaps some organised farming and fishing for tourists and local visitors could be attempted. For a price, they could sample coconut juice, tap rubber, fish for prawns and sea bass, visit the *kelong* and villagers' homes, sample locally harvested vegetables and fruits and seafood. There is also potential for conducted nature and cycling tours as long as the original atmosphere of Ubin is retained.

Pulau Ubin should be preserved in its entirety as it is the last reminder of a bygone era that shaped modern Singapore.

Managing the Adventure

Over a thousand visitors troop to Pulau Ubin on weekends. Besides the avid nature lover, the idyllic island is also an ideal refuge for the sporting, the adventurous and the stressed. Unlike "manicured" lawns and parks, the relatively undisturbed greenery in Ubin creates more challenge and offers unusual glimpses of wildlife.

Ubin's popularity as an outdoor retreat and repository of wildlife may be what saves the island from being developed for residential purposes. But Ubin runs the risk of being a victim of its own popularity. Outdoor activities, if not managed properly, can actually lead to great destruction.

Setting aside space

A large part of Pulau Ubin, covering about 549 hectares, is designated as the Pulau Ubin Recreation Area. The National Parks Board (NParks) promotes the use of this Recreation Area for compatible outdoor recreation, conservation, research and education.

Outdoor activities such as cycling, camping, hiking, picnicking, treasure hunts, nature walks and fishing are actively promoted. Basic public amenities such as an Information Kiosk, toilets and map boards were provided in 1997. In an ongoing effort to improve the safety and conduct of outdoor activities, old rickety bridges have also been replaced with proper ones and safety features such as road humps, signage and railings have been installed. Additional facilities being planned for include rain shelters, lookout points, campsites and interpretative storyboards.

Above: Rock climbing is not without its dangers. Proper attire and gear and training under professionals will reduce the risks. This task is undertaken by a select group of individuals of the Outward Bound Singapore but the risk of loosened granite at the edges has placed abseiling activities at the quarries on hold.

Opposite: Defying death at the HDB Granite Quarry. The overpowering surge of adrenalin had many youngsters seeking the thrills of plunging into the cool waters from a height — safety is often well forgotten. This is discouraged by NParks as many unseen dangers lurk and there have been fatalities.

Above and below: A NParks' officer handling a Banded Krait (*Bungarus fasciatus*) that was probably run over by a vehicle. Another staff measures a bat caught by one of the mist nets set up during a night survey.

Right: Schools and activity groups often plan hiking and camping trips for youths on the island. Besides the whiff of fresh air, these youths are exposed to skills in interaction and teamwork.

To monitor the development and oversee the day-to-day management of the Recreation Area, officers and rangers are stationed on the island. Each day, the rangers will patrol the island to advise and assist visitors. Management staff will also be on their rounds to look out for trees and branches that may fall and endanger visitors. Any hornet's nest or bee-hive spotted along the designated public accesses will be removed. Public amenities are inspected on a daily basis to ensure that they are clean and in good working condition.

The community is involved in NParks' outreach and research programmes. To increase nature awareness and appreciation, officers train volunteers to conduct nature walks, and work with grassroots organisations to conduct outreach activities. Volunteers are also involved in ongoing research and monitoring programmes in Pulau Ubin. Although some data on the island's diverse fauna is available, a survey has been initiated to provide new baseline information for conservation into the new millennium. Similar surveys are being initiated to document the plant life to update earlier studies. Areas with important habitats for indigenous plants and animals will be identified, and strategies and programmes formulated to preserve and protect them.

Staying on Ubin

Noordin Beach is a mandatory stop for those looking for an undisturbed stretch of beach. The number

of dome-shaped tents in a multitude of colour attests to its popularity as a camping site. Washroom and toilet facilities are available. The vast panoramic view of the Johor coastline appears more tempting; it is a wonder why the elephant decided to swim over.

Mamam Beach faced serious soil erosion but shore protection measures by the National Parks Board in 1999 helped retain the site. A new campsite was also established and these changes cost around $500,000. Ringed by wooden railings, the sandy beach is popular with campers. Benches with attached tables are provided for.

Unfortunately, facilities have been sometimes vandalised or damage through carelessness with barbecue fires. On Ubin, the natural and man-made both need to be protected from the carelessness and callousness of some members of the public.

For those who do not fancy camping, but wish to stay on Ubin, the Ubin Lagoon Resort opened on May 2000 and $25 million was invested in it to make it the ultimate adventure experience in Singapore. Hopefully, these offerings will be kept as spartan as possible so that one has time to experience what Ubin has to offer.

Above: The island is popular due to the convenience of its proximity to the mainland and the presence of the vast areas of "green solitude".

Outward Bound Singapore

Outward Bound Singapore (OBS) embodies the spirit of adventure and has been pivotal in the training of young Singaporeans to meet the changing needs of society. It offers a series of programmes which uses the natural environment to enable individuals to manage fear, stressful situations and cope effectively with the unknown.

The programmes are also excellent for nurturing team spirit and for building mental tenacity. Although teenagers and young adults are the school's main focus, lately, private organisations see it paramount to engage their recruits and even senior management staff in the school's many programmes. Programmes include activities such as abseiling, jumping from jetties into deep water, kayaking and rafting and aerial obstacle courses.

The OBS has helped almost 153,000 participants (from 1967 to 1999) to discover and develop their potential. It currently employs 48 trainers and 46 administrative and support staff.

Sited on the northwestern section of Ubin, OBS aims to help people develop confidence and teamwork through outdoor adventure. The sea, the cliffs of the quarry lakes and the secondary forest in its vicinity make Ubin a natural choice for training.

Fishing

Towards the west are some good fishing spots. Anglers often camp overnight at these sites. Fish in the area include Mullet, Sea Bass, Estuarine Catfish, Grouper, Selar, Frogfish, Four-striped Cardinalfish and Flower Crabs. Unfortunately, the occasional Sea Horse is also caught. The mangroves around Ubin are excellent grounds for the many fish species to grow and propagate. But care needs to be exercised, for one person drowned, slipping off a wooden jetty after a fishing trip.[43] The lack of prawns or squid for bait is not a problem. One can dig for sea worms in the estuarine areas for use as bait.

Cycling

Kiddy bikes, tandem bikes, tricycles and mountain bikes — they are all for rent. A casual joy ride is what many come to Ubin for. With the wind on your face and in your hair and no heavy traffic, cycling on Ubin can be relaxed. Going downhill is even more fun! But do take care as some corners are quite sharp and the brakes on rental bikes cannot always stop a speeding bicycle quickly enough. But the serious cyclist brings his or her own bicycle, equipped with the latest suspension systems and togged out in the flashiest apparel.

There are simple rules for biking on the island, like single file cycling, giving way to the taxis and motorcyclists, taking care with gravel ground espe-

Above left: Fishing with just a hook and line can be exciting at the *kelong*. Memories of such activities are not easily forgotten.

Above right: Patience is often rewarded. The Orange Mud Crab (*Scylla olivacea*) that was lured by bait over a net trap had its claws and legs hopelessly entangled. This crab is abundant in mangrove habitats. Fried with chilli, pepper or just plain steaming, these crabs make a good meal.

Left: The punishing uphill slopes and the wind against one's face as one careens downhill — these are the thrills of biking over uneven terrain.

cially on turning and riding at sensible speeds. When riding over bridges, it is important to focus ahead. A non-swimmer drowned when she fell into a river after colliding with another fellow cyclist on a makeshift bridge on 31 January 1995. Wider bridges with reinforcements were constructed and railings have been fitted over Sungei Puaka and Sungei Jelutong to prevent accidents.[44]

When in season, cycling under durian trees without helmets can be an unnerving experience. The ripe thorny fruits pack quite a wallop if you are in line with its descent. Stay away from these trees during stormy weather. Likewise, it is prudent not to camp under coconut trees. Towards the west, cyclists are increasingly dismayed by signboards that indicate the extended boundaries of the Outward Bound Singapore.

Sea sports

The surrounding seas are wonderful for canoeing and a stop at Pulau Sekudu (popularly called Frog Island) for a picnic is an ideal outing. The many rivers are also tempting for those who wish to take a slow boat ride.

However, rafting in the rivers of Ubin is not a simple matter. This is fraught with dangers due to the strong currents and swirl pools created by the changing tides at the water-gates. Two teenagers drowned in one such unfortunate accident at Sungei Jelutong.[45] Danger also lurks at the granite quarries where the ponds appeal to swimmers and divers. A boy drowned when he fell into one of the ponds in March 1996.

Sightseeing on Ubin

A trail leads up to Bukit Puaka (75 m) or Puaka Hill, which is the highest hill on the island and overlooks the Ubin Granite Quarry. But fences have been erected around most of the quarries. Quarry lakes are now off-limits. In the past, daredevils dived off cliffs and swam in the quarry lakes. This is often fraught with danger as the waters are less buoyant and fatalities are a reality. Rising water levels have also drowned some of the paths and the depths are uneven.

Below: OBS participants practise the finer points of handling a canoe in open water, preparing for a longer trip around Ubin itself.

Left: The view from Puaka Hill showcases the jade-coloured waters of the HDB Quarry lake. Nature restores beauty even when the actions of man scar the earth.

Below: Ubin offers premium sites for bird-watching. If one is lucky enough, the Mangrove Pitta might swoop into view. Even more rare is the Cinnamon-headed Green Pigeon. Bird-watchers willingly forgo their precious early Sunday mornings just to catch a glimpse of the special feathered denizens of Ubin.

Viewing the waters from the quarry edge is a precarious experience due to the possibility of loosening granite because of the constant erosion. Hence the lakes were cordoned off to prevent any mishap. It is hoped that free access be granted in future where one can view the quarry but with safety measures already in place. Perhaps the quarry lakes can be transformed into areas where water sports can be encouraged. Fishes were once released into the waters of the disused quarry by Mr Goh Chok Tong, then First Deputy Prime Minister.[46] Regulated freshwater fishing could also be a possibility.

On a short walk from the jetty to behind the Civil Service Club chalets, one can ramble through some fruit and coconut plantation to the mangrove forests. Students on field trips have much to learn about the mangrove ecosystem. Nature rambles to more distant areas expose these students to the different habitats and their importance.

Some will seek fulfilment in nature. But the

Above: Former Member of Parliament, Mr Ho Kah Leong, painting a *kampung* scene. He had been drawn to the idyllic island for the past 15 years and lamented its impending fate (*The Straits Times*, 8 October 1999).

Below: Taking a walk on the wild side. Many schools have sought the wilderness of Ubin to imbibe values, nurture the love for nature and to expose schoolchildren to more demanding physical activities.

island is a premium place for bird-watching. Eco-tourists have gone eagerly to Ubin, seeking out the many birds. Bird-watching trips organised by the Nature Society are often overwhelmingly subscribed. Many are pleasantly surprised with the number of species of birds that can be found on the island.

Inspired by nature, local artists have been drawn to Ubin for the past 15 years.[47] The *kampung* dwellings, the landscapes, the tranquil seclusion of the quarry lakes, the lushness of the flora — are all perfect subjects for artistic expression. They were able to showcase their work in an exhibition entitled "Beautiful Ubin" at the Selegie Gallery.[48]

Some guided walks or cycling trips would be a perfect start to the understanding of the wilderness of Ubin. On the heavily trodden paths, mammal

encounters are almost non-existent as most of these creatures are nocturnal, with the exception of an occasional squirrel or shy Long-tailed Macaque (*Macaca fascicularis*). Birds are more noticeable, but late mornings or early afternoons are often poor for bird sightings. Enlisting the services from the birding experts of the Nature Society would be the best way to appreciate the bird life on the island. Appreciating nature takes some effort and preparation.

Community action

Safety guidelines jointly published by NParks, OBS, the Siglap Citizens' Consultative Committee and the Pulau Ubin Community Centre Management Committee are timely and are available at the NParks Information Kiosk. To reduce accidents, visitors are constantly reminded not to take the wilderness of Ubin for granted and should practise environmentally friendly habits.

NParks and the People's Association organised a family excursion on the island where there were fun and games, and participants were brought closer with mother nature. About a thousand residents from the Northeast and Marine Parade Community Development Council (CDC) took part.[49]

The "Ubin Discovery Trail", launched under NParks' Adopt-a-Park Programme and adopted by the Marine Parade CDC and the Boys' Brigade in Singapore on 21 May 2000, saw more than 200 children

Left: Nothing beats the Great Outdoors, especially by the campfire — with good music, great friends and a barbecue under the night sky. Pulau Ubin is a perfect getaway.

participating in nature walks and learning about the natural heritage of Ubin. The 4-km trail meandered across coconut and rubber plantations and mangrove forests. NParks trained volunteers from the Boys' Brigade and the Siglap Youth Executive Committee members as nature guides.[50]

More regular tours for children will be organised and children exposed to nature may value the more intangible and less materialistic aspects of life — a balance necessary in a competitive society that stresses a lot on self-interests. NParks together with the Singapore American School and the Singapore Association of the Visually Handicapped co-adopted the Sensory Trail in Pulau Ubin on 15 April 2000 and the occasion was graced by the Honourable Mr Steven J. Green, the American Ambassador to Singapore.

The trail included a garden site with a diversity of vegetables and aromatic plants and complete with signs in Braille and English. The idea was first hatched in 1995 by Catherine Frazier (SAVE — Students Against Violating the Environment) and Evelyn Eng-Lim (NSS) in 1995. The trail will provide access for the enjoyment of the visually handicapped in an otherwise disadvantaged world for them.

Understanding nature goes beyond our textbooks. Enjoying the great outdoors together is an excellent way to build up camaraderie and family unity. Youth learn skills in people interaction outside school and these help them focus on real issues of a real world — that is, it takes a lot of effort to live harmoniously together and that the issue of the handicapped is also the issue of the able.

125

Ours to Treasure

"It makes far better sense to reshape ourselves to fit a finite planet than to attempt to reshape the planet to fit our infinite wants."

— Professor David Orr in an address for a Graduating Class of Arkansas College, USA, 1990.

The island of Ubin takes a breather, relieved after the weekend assault. She waits for the following weekend, wondering whether she will be razed to the ground and whether she will be spared a few more years. The prospect of having four million people in Singapore is daunting and has driven town-planners to the shores of Ubin to look for alternative housing sites.

Ubin is our last rural retreat in Singapore. Take away the wilderness and the special denizens of Ubin, you take away the tenuous link between people and nature. The very reason why Ubin draws a huge crowd, especially on weekends and holidays, is obvious. The proximity and accessibility to the island is an advantage. For those who need to seek some undisturbed solitude, away from the shopping malls, away from the close-built blocks of housing estates and away from the stresses of work without going overseas, Pulau Ubin is the alternative.

The different birdcalls are music to the ears. For riding away with minimal fuss and burning excess calories to keep fit, Ubin's many uneven trails are ideal. The need to connect with the untamed wilderness is an added seduction; for the forests of Ubin will be a feast for the senses. No road rage or road bullies, no reactive altercations, no paper chase, no "boxed-in living" — just simple pleasures. A getaway island, an adventure island, an island in the sun, a nature island — Pulau Ubin is all these and more.

Where can one find another paradise like Ubin? Far away in another land, far away in another time in our history. The spate of letters to the local papers from 28 September to 8 October 1999 strongly urging the authorities to leave Ubin's history and natural beauty alone will hopefully will not be in vain.

Above: Paradise now — but for how much longer?

Opposite: This *kampung house*, if left undisturbed, will remain a showcase for future generations. It is a living cultural lesson that is in need of conservation and protection.

127

Above: Once a winter visitor, the Dollarbird or Broadbilled Roller (*Eurystomus orientalis*) is actively breeding on the island. Commonly seen perched on top of dead coconut trees, hunting sorties are often impressive aerial displays where insects are caught on the wing.

Some of the appeals against the development started way before that.[51] Besides the loss of our natural heritage, what about our cultural heritage? What about the last of the traditional Chinese villages and Malay *kampung*? Are they not important to be conserved for future generations? These were the humble beginnings of our young nation. The loss of the natural and the cultural — what a price for progress.

The challenge for Singaporeans will be how to balance the demands of population growth with needs for a closer association with nature. How can the forests and mangroves in Pulau Ubin be retained to support ecosystems that enable wildlife to survive? And how does one establish the green corridors that will be essential to sustain this wildlife?

In urbanised Singapore, where developments and nature conservation often run counter to each other, a balance has to be found. The increasing environmental awareness around the world has compelled many to look again at their lives and future generations, for these issues matter to many.

For the Singaporean, Ubin gives one a sense of identity, a sense of ownership and a sense of responsibility to partake in its destiny. Once the first flats are built on the island, it is hard to imagine how the fragmented island can serve its purpose as a natural heritage. Artificial pockets of greenery will not replace the natural heritage. Once dismantled, we cannot adequately restore the wilderness. Ubin's natural heritage should be retained so that the generations that follow us can be enriched by the historical and natural connections. Public concern about the developments on Ubin has been roused but will their pleas be heard?

Some of the trades such as tropical fish, prawn and poultry farming and local fruit production could be retained for young Singaporeans as a living experience from the past. Some of the homes could be renovated according to previous designs and retained for the village and *kampung* experience. If only Ubin's inhabitants could be allowed to stay instead of being resettled. The current transition before the big transformation is disturbing enough for many. Ubin needs its *kampung* folk to retain its charm.

Standing guard to the entrance of the island is a granite rock that has an uncanny resemblance to a rhinoceros. Shaped by the natural elements, it will continue to weather the storms of nature, but I am not sure if Pulau Ubin can weather the storms of progress. The rhinoceros is endangered, but our obvious indifference to its dwindling numbers is alarming. In many ways, this rhinoceros rock symbolises Ubin's plight. Which way will we go? For me, there is only one answer.

Pulau Ubin is ours to treasure.

Left: This picture was taken in June 1996 near Kampung Tengah. It shows a woman whom regular bird-watchers knew as Ah Gu's mother. Further behind her on the dirt track, a group of boys try to get some coconuts with a pole.

Ah Gu and his mother no longer live on Ubin, having probably resettled on the mainland. That's understandable, some might say. But Ah Gu's move has a deeper meaning. Is it the tacit acknowledgement that life on Ubin must inevitably change? Or is it just that the generations have changed? That the simple life in harmony with nature is no longer possible — or desirable?

If a way of life for people must pass, then so be it. But the same cannot be said for the plants and creatures that still remain.

Map of Pulau Ubin

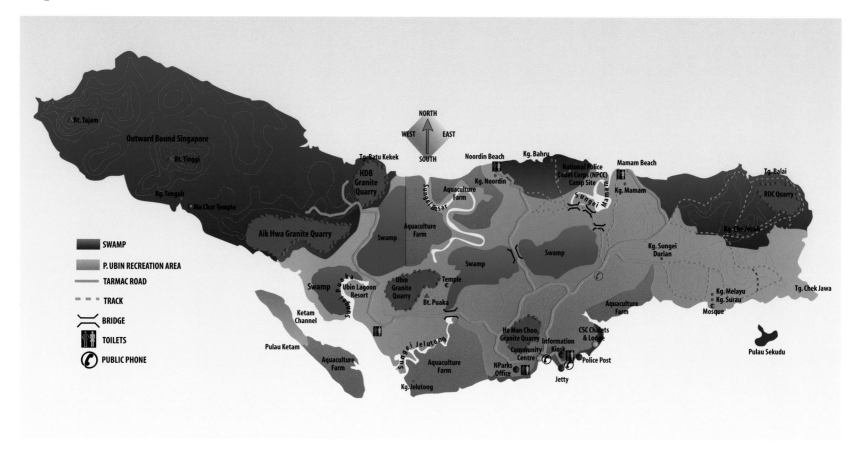

Legend:
- SWAMP
- P. UBIN RECREATION AREA
- TARMAC ROAD
- TRACK
- BRIDGE
- TOILETS
- PUBLIC PHONE

Notes to the chapters

1   *Lianhe Zhao Bao*, 23/7/90.

2   *Lianhe Zhao Bao*, 12/2/95.

3   *Lianhe Zhao Bao*, 5/3/95.

4   *Lianhe Zhao Bao*, 12/2/95.

5   *Lianhe Zhao Bao*, 23/7/90.

6   *Lianhe Zhao Bao*, 18/8/85, 5/1/88.

7   *The Straits Times*, 7/4/81.

8   *Lianhe Wanbao*, 14/3/87.

9   *Sin Ming Daily*, 27/10/87.

10 *The Straits Times*, 13/9/88.

11 *The Straits Times*, 15/2/95.

12 *The Straits Times*, 7/8/84.

13 *The Straits Times*, 2/5/95.

14 *The Straits Times*, 14/10/99.

15 *Changi*, November 1993.

16 *The New Paper*, 2/3/91.

17 *The Sunday Times*, 10/3/91.

18 *The New Paper*, 4/12/90.

19 *The Straits Times*, 30/4/98.

20 *The New Paper*, 6/8/91.

21 *The Straits Times*, 25/12/99.

22 *The Straits Times*, 3/10/97; 7/10/97.

23 *The Straits Times*, 11/10/62.

24 *The Straits Times*, 15/2/95.

25 *The Straits Times*, 1/4/97.

26 *The Straits Times*, 1/4/97.

27 *The Straits Times*, 7/3/91.

28 *The Sunday Times*, 10/3/91.

29 *The Straits Times*, 30/4/98.

30 *The Straits Times*, 6/7/99.

31 *The New Straits Times*, 14/3/99.

32 *The Straits Times*, 28/2/99.

33 *The Sunday Times*, 6/4/97.

34 *The Sunday Times*, 15/9/91.

35 *The Straits Times*, 20/5/92.

36 *The Straits Times*, 20/5/99.

37 *The Straits Times*, 10/2/99; 14/10/99.

38 *The Straits Times*, 16/11/99.

39 *The Straits Times*, 15/2/2000.

40 *The Straits Times*, 27/2/98.

41 *The Straits Times*, 16/9/91.

42 *The Straits Times*, 7/5/97.

43 *The Straits Times*, 25/12/99.

44 *The Straits Times*, 4/3/95.

45 *The Straits Times*, 8/2/99.

46 *The Straits Times*, 9/10/90.

47 *The Straits Times*, 15/1/2000.

48 *The Straits Times*, 15/1/2000.

49 *The Straits Times*, 24/1/2000.

50 *The Straits Times*, 26/5/2000.

51 *The Straits Times*, 2/3/91; 15/3/92; 20/5/92.

The Plants of Pulau Ubin — A Checklist

This list of vascular plants is based primarily on a report Turner et al (1992). Additional plants collected by staff of the Herbarium, Singapore Botanical Gardens were added to the list.

A = Alien, C = Common, E = Exotic, N = Endangered, R = Rare,
S = Escape, V = vulnerable, X = extinct, ? = Unknown status

1 LYCOPODOPHYTA	
Lycopodiaceae	
Lycopodiella cernua (L.) Pic. Serm.	C
2 FILICINOPHYTA	
Adiantaceae	
Adiantum latifolium Lamk.	A
Taenitis blechnoides (Willd.) Sw.	N
Aspleniaceae	
Asplenium nidus L.	C
Blechnaceae	
Blechnum orientale L.	V
Stenochlaena palustris (Burm.) Bedd.	C
Davalliaceae	
Davallia denticulata (Burm.) Mett.	C
Dennstaedtiaceae	
Lindsaea ensifolia Sw.	V
Gleicheniaceae	
Dicranopteris linearis (Burm. f.) Underw.	C
Hemionitidacceae	
Pityrogramma calomelanos (L.) Link	A
Oleandraceae	
Nephrolepis biserrata (Sw.) Schott	C
Parkeriaceae	
Ceratopteris thalictroides (L.) Brongn.	C
Polypodiaceae	
Drynaria quercifolia (L.) J. Sm.	C
Phymatosorus scolopendria (Burm.) Pic Serm.	C
Platycerium coronarium (Koenig) Desv.	C
Pyrrosia longifolia (Burm.) Morton	C
Pyrrosia piloselloides (L.) Price	C
Pteridaceae	
Acrostichum aureum L.	C
Acrostichum speciosum Willd.	C
Pteridium caudatum (L.) Maxon	
ssp. *yarrabense* (Domin) Parris	V
Pteris semipinnata L.	R
Pteris vittata L.	C
SchizaeceaeL	
Lygodium circinnatum (Burm. f.) Sw.	V
Lygodium microphyllum (Cav.) R. Br.	C
Schizaea digitata (L.) Sw.	C
3 GNETOPHYTA	
Gnetaceae	
Gnetum macrostachyum Hook.	V
4 MAGNOLIOPHYTA	
Acanthaceae	
Acanthus ebracteatus Vahl	R
Acanthus ilicifolius L.	R
Acanthus volubilis Wall.	R
Andrographis paniculata (Burm. f.) Nees	A
Asystasia nemorum Ness	C
Hemigraphis primulifolia (Nees) Vill	A
Thunbergia fragrans Roxb.	C
Thunbergia grandiflora Roxb.	A
Agavaceae	
Sansevieria trifasciata Prain	S

Aizoaceae	
Sesuvium portulacastrum L.	R
Amaranthaceae	
Celosia argentea L.	A
Cyathula prostrata (L.) Bl.	R
Gomphrena globosa L.	S
Anacardiaceae	
Anacardium occidentale L.	A
Bouea macrophylla Griff	R
Buchanania arborescens (Bl.) Bl.	R
Campnosperma auriculatum (Bl.) Hook. f.	R
Mangifera indica L.	S
Annonaceae	
Desmos dasymaschala (Bl.) Safford	R
Uvaria hirsuta Jack	R
Apocynaceae	
Allamanda cathartica L.	S
Alstonia angustiloba Miq.	C
Alstonia spathulata Bl.	V
Catharanthus roseus (L.) G. Don	A
Cerbera odollam Gaertn.	R
Araceae	
Alocasia macrorrhizos (L.) G. Don	A
Colocasia esculenta (L.) Schott	C
Dieffenbachia seguine (Jacq.) Schott	S
Epipremnum pinnatum (L.) Engl.	X
Homalomena griffithii (Schott) Hook. f.	V
Araliaceae	
Arthrophyllum diversifolium Bl.	C
Polyscias fruticosa (L.) Harms	S
Schefflera elliptica (Bl.) Harms	R
Asclepiadaceae	
Dischidia major (Vahl) Merr.	R
Dischidia nummularia R. Br.	C
Hoya parasitica (Roxb.) Wall. ex. Wight	R
Avicenniaceae	
Avicennia alba Bl.	C
Avicennia officinalis Bl.	R
Avicennia rumphiana Hall. f.	R
Bignoniaceae	
Spathodea campanulata Beauv.	A
Dolichandrone spathacea (L.f.) K. Schum.	E
Bombacaceae	
Durio zibethinus J. Murray	S
Boraginaceae	
Cordia cylindristachya Roem. & Schult.	A
Heliotropium indicum L.	C
Bromeliaceae	
Ananas comosus (L.) Merr. cv. Mauritius	S
Cannaceae	
Canna indica L.	A
Capparaceae	
Cleome rutidosperma DC.	A
Caricaceae	
Carica papaya L.	S
Casuarinaceae	
Casuarina equisetifolia J. R. & G. Forst.	C
Celastraceae	
Salacia chinensis L.	V
Combretaceae	
Lumnitzera littorea (Jack) Voight	R
Lumnitzera racemosa Willd.	R
Terminalia catappa L.	C
Commelinaceae	
Commelina diffusa Burm f.	C
Compositae	
Acmella uliginosa (Sw.) Cass.	R

Ageratum conyzoides L.	A
Bidens pilosa L.	A
Blumea balsamifera (L.) DC.	R
Conyza honariensis (L.) Cronquist	C
Eclipta prostrata (L.) L.	C
Elephantopus scaber L.	C
Emilia sonchifolia (L.) DC. ex Wight	C
Gynura procumbens (Lour.) Merr.	R
Mikania cordata (Burm. f.) B. L. Robinson	A
Pluchea indica (L.) Less.	R
Sparganophorus sparganophora (L.) C. Jeffrey	A
Synedrella nodiflora (L.) Gaertn.	A
Tridax procumbens L.	A
Vernonia cinerea (L.) Less.	C
Wedelia biflora (L.) DC.	C
Wedelia trilobata (L.) Hitch	A
Youngia japonica (L.) DC.	C
Connaraceae	
Cnestis palala (Lour.) Merr.	R
Convolvulaceae	
Erycibe tomentosa Bl.	C
Ipomoea aquatica Forsk.	C
Ipomoea batatas (L.) Lamk.	S
Ipomoea brasilennsis (L.) Sweet	C
Ipomoea cairica (L.) Sweet	A
Merremia tridentala (L.) Hallier. f.	C
Cuscuta australis R. Br.	R
Cucurbitaceae	
Cucumis sativa L.	S
Mukia maderaspatana (L.) M. J. Roem.	A
Cyperaceae	
Bulbostylis barbata (Rottb.) Clarke	C
Cyperus aromaticus (Ridi.) Mattf. & Kuk	A
Cyperus compactus Retz	R
Cyperus compressus L.	C
Cyperus cyperinus (Retz.) Valck. Sur.	C
Cyperus haspan L.	C
Cyperus javanicus Houtt.	C
Cyperus kyllingia Endl.	C
Cyperrus pilosus Vahl	R
Cyperus trialatus (Bocck.) Kern	R
Fimbristylis cymosa R. Br.	R
Fimbristylis dichotoma (L.) Vahl	R
Fimbristylis gtiffithii Boeck.	R
Fimbristylis polytrichoides (Retz.) R. Br.	R
Fimbristylis schoenoides (Retz.) Vahl	R
Hypolytrum nemorum (Vahl) Spreng.	R
Scleria corymbosa Roxb.	R
Scleria levis Retz.	C
Thoracostachyum bancanum (Miq.) Kurz.	R
Dilleniaceae	
Dillenia suffruticosa (Griff.) Mart.	C
Tetracera indica (Christm. & Panz.) Merr.	C
Dioscoreaceae	
Dioscorea glabra Roxb.	R
Dioscorea laurifolia Wall. ex Hook. f.	C
Elaeocarpaceae	
Elaeocarpus ferrugineus (Jack) Steud.	R
Elaeocarpus pedunculatus Wall. ex Mast.	R
Muntingia calabura L.	A
Eriocaulaceae	
Eriocaulon longifolium Nees	C
Erythroxylaceae	
Erythroxylum cuneatum (Miq.) Kurz.	R
Euphorbiaceae	
Antidesma velutinosum Bl.	R
Baccaurea motleyana (M.A.) M.A.	S

Breynia coronata Hook. f.	R
Bridelia stipularis (L.) Bl.	R
Claoxylon indicum (Reinw. ex Bl.) Endl. ex Hassk.	C
Codiaeum variegatum (L.) Bl.	S
Croton hirtus L′ Heritier	A
Euphorbia hirta L.	A
Excoecaria agallocha L.	R
Glochidion superbum Baill.	R
Hevea brasiliensis (Willd. ex A. Juss.) M.A.	A
Macaranga conifera M.A.	C
Macaranga gigantea (Rchb. f. & Zoll.) M.A.	C
Macaranga griffithiana M.A.	R
Macaranga heynei I.M. Johnston	C
Macaranga hypoleuca (Rchb. f. & Zoll.) M.A.	C
Macaranga triloba (Bl.) M.A.	C
Mallotus paniculatus (Lamk.) M.A.	C
Manihot esculenta Crantz	A
Manihot glaziovii M.A.	A
Phyllanthus acidus (L.) Skeels	S
Phyllanthus amarus Schum. & Thonn.	A
Phyllanthus debilis Klein ex Willd.	A
Phyllanthus urinaria L.	C
Ricinus communis L.	A
Sapium discolor (Champ. Ex Benth.) M.A.	C
Suregada multiflora (Juss.) Baill.	R

Flagellariaceae
Flagellaria indica L.	R

Goodeniaceae
Scaevola sericea Vahl	C

Gramineae
Axonopus compressus (Swartz) Beauv.	A
Bambusa glaucescens (Willd.) Sieb.	S
Bambusa vulgaris Scharad. ex Wendl	S
Centotheca latifolia (Osb.) Trin.	R
Chloris barbata Swartz	A
Chrysopogon aciculatus (Retz.) Trin.	C
Coix lacryma-jobi L.	A
Cynodon dactylon (L.) Pers.	C
Cyrtococcum accrescens (Trin.) Stapf	C
Dactyloctenium aegyptium (L.) P. Beauv.	C
Dendrocalamus asper (Schult.) Backer ex Heyne	S
Digitaria ciliaris (Retz.) Koel.	C
Echinochloa colona (L.) Link	C
Eleusine indica (L.) Gaertn.	C
Eragrostis pilosa (L.) P. Beauv.	R
Gigantochloa levis (Blanco) Merr.	S
Imperata cylindrica (L.) P. Beauv.	C
Ischaemum ciliare Retz.	C
Ischaemum muticum L.	C
Melinis repens (Willd.) Zizka	A
Mnesithea glandulosa (Trin.) Koning & Sosef	C
Panicum maximum Jacq.	A
Paspalum conjugatum Berg.	A
Paspalum orbiculare Forst. f.	C
Penniseturn polystachyon (L.) Schult.	A
Pogonatherum paniceum (Lamk.) Hack.	C
Saccharum arundinaceum Retz.	C
Sporobolus indicus (L.) R. Br.	C
Thysanolaena latifolia (Roxb. Ex Hornem.) Honda	A
Zoysia matrella (L.) Merr.	C

Guttiferae
Calophyllum inophyllum L.	R
Calophyllum pulcherrimum Wall. ex Choisy	R
Garcinia mangostana L.	S
Garcinia nigrolineata Planch. ex T. Anders.	R

Hypoxidaceae
Curculigo latifolia Dryand. in Ait.	R

Ixonanthaceae
Ixonanthes reticulata Jack	C

Labiatae
Hyptis brevipes Poit.	A
Hyptis capitata Jacq.	A
Hyptis suaveolens (L.) Poit.	A
Leucas zeylanica (L.) R. Br.	R
Ocimum basilicum L.	R
Ocimum sanctum L.	R

Lauraceae
Cassytha filiformis L.	C
Cinnamomum iners Reinw. ex Bl.	C
Neolitsea zeylanica Merr.	R

Lecaceae
eea indica (Burm. f.) Merr.	R

Leguminosae
Abrus precatorius L.	A
Acacia auriculiformis A. Cunn. ex Benth.	A
Acacia mangium Willd.	S
Alysicarpus vaginalis (L.) DC.	R
Andira inermis (W. Wright) H.B.K. ex DC.	S
Archidendron clypearia (Jack) I. Nielsen	R
Caesalpinia crista L.	R
Calopogoniurn mucunoides Desv.	A
Canavalia cathartica Thou.	C
Centrasema pubescens Benth.	A
Chamaecrista mimosoides (L.) Greene	A
Chamaecrista nictinans (L.) Moench	A
Clitoria lauriflora Poir.	A
Crotalaria pallida Ait.	A
Dalbergia candenatensis (Dennst.) Prain	R
Derris elliptica (Roxb.) Benth.	S
Derris trifoliata Lour.	C
Desmodium heterocarpon (L.) DC.	R
Desmodium heterophyllum (Willd.) DC.	C
Desmodium umbellatum (L.) DC.	C
Entada spiralis Ridl.	R
Intsia bijuga (Colebr.) O. Ktze.	R
Mimosa diplotricha C. Wright ex Sauvalle	A
Mimosa pigra L.	A
Mimosa pudica L.	A
Neptunia plena (L.) Benth.	A
Peltophorum pterocarpum (DC.) Backer ex Heyne	V
Pterocarpus indicus Willd.	S
Senna alata (L.) Roxb.	A
Pueraria lobata (Willd.) Ohwi	A

Lemnaceae
Lenna perpusilla Torrey	C

Liliaceae
Cordyline fruticosa (L.) A. Chev.	S
Dianella ensifolia (L.) DC.	C
Gloriosa superba L.	S
Dracaena maingayi Hook. f	V

Linaceae
Indorouchera griffithiana (Planch.) Hallier f.	R

Loganiaceae
Fagraea fragrans Roxb.	C
Fagraea racemosa Jack ex Wall.	N

Loranthaceae
Dendrophthoe pentandra (L.) Miq.	C
Macrosolen cochinchinensis (Lour.) Tiegh.	C
Scurrula parasitica L.	N

Magnoliaceae
Michelia champaca L.	S

Malpighiaceae
Tristellateia australasiae A. Rich.	V

Malvaceae
Hibiscus rosa-sinensis L.	S
Hibiscus tiliaceus L.	C
Sida rhombifolia L.	C
Thespesia populnea (L.) Soland. ex Correa	R
Urena lobata L.	C

Melastomataceae
Clidemia hirta D. Don	A
Dissochaeta gracilis (Jack) Bl.	R
Melastoma malabathricum L.	C
Memecylon edule Roxb.	R
Memecylon edule Roxb. var. *ovatum* Clarke	R

Meliaceae
Xylocarpus granatum Koen.	R

Menispermaceae
Fibraurea tinctoria Lour.	R
Limacia scandens Lour.	R

Moraceae
Artocarpus dadah Miq.	R
Artocarpus integer (Thunb.) Merr.	S
Artocarpus heterophyllus Lamk.	S
Ficus aurata Miq.	R
Ficus fistulosa Reinw. ex Bl.	C
Ficus grossularioides Burm. f.	C
Ficus heteropleura Bl.	C
Ficus microcarpa L.f.	C
Ficus variegata Bl.	C
Ficus virens Ait. var. *glabella* (Bl.) Corner	R
Streblus elongatus (Miq.) Corner	R
Trophis scandens (Lour.)Hk. & Arnott	E

Musaceae
Musa cultivar	E

Myricaceae
Myrica esculenta Buch.-Ham.	C

Myristicaceae
Knema globularia Warb.	X

Myrsinaceae
Ardisia crenata Sims	R
Ardisia ellipitica Thunb.	R
Embelia ribes Burm.	R

Myrtaceae
Eugenia jambos L.	S
Eugenia longiflora (Presl) F. – Vill.	C
Eugenia palembanica (Miq.) Merr.	R
Eugenia spicata Lamk.	C
Psidium guajava L.	S
Rhodamnia cinerea Jack	C
Rhodomyrtus tomentosa (Ait.) Hassk.	C
Tristaniopsis whiteana (Griff.) Wilson & Waterhouse	S

Nepenthaceae
Nepenthes ampullaria Jack	R
Nepenthes gracilis Korth.	C

Olaceae
Ximenia americana L.	R

Oleaceae
Jasminum sambac Ait	A

Onagraceae
Ludwigia hyssopifolia (G. Don) Exell	C

Opiliaceae
Cansjera rheedii J.F. Gmel	V
Champereia manillana (Bl.) Merr.	C

Orchidaceae
Bromheadia finlaysoniana (Lindl.) Rchb. f.	C
Dendrobium crumenatum Sw.	C

Neuwiedia veratrifolia Bl.	N
Spathoglotis plicata Bl.	C
Thrixspermum amplexicaule (Bl.) Rchb. f.	N
Vanilla griffiithii Rchb. f.	R
Oxalidaceae	
Oxalis barrelieri L.	A
Oxalis corniculata L.	A
Palmae	
Arenga pinnata (Wurmb) Merr.	S
Calamus erinaceus (Becc.) Dransf.	V
Caryota mitis Lour.	C
Cocos nucifera L.	A
Licuala spinosa Wurmb	R
Nypa fruticans Wurmb	R
Oncosperma tigillarium (Jack) Ridl.	R
Pandanaceae	
Pandanus amarylifolius Roxb.	S
Pandanus odoratissimus L. f.	C
Pandanus yvanii Solms.	R
Passifloraceae	
Passiflora foetida L.	A
Passiflora laurifolia L.	A
Passiflora suberosa L.	A
Pedaliaceae	
Sesamum radiatum Schum.	A
Piperaceae	
Peperomia pellucida (L.) H.B.K.	A
Piper betle L.	S
Piper sarmentosurn Roxb. ex Hunter	C
Plantaginaceae	
Plantago major L.	C
Portulacaceae	
Talinum paniculatum (Jacq.) Gaertn.	A
Rhamnaceae	
Colubrina asiatica L. ex Brongn.	R
Rhizophoraceae	
Bruguiera cylindrica (L.) Bl.	R
Bruguiera gymnorrhiza (L.) Lamk.	R
Ceriops tagal (Perr.) C.B. Robinson	R
Gynotroches axillaris Bl.	R
Rhizophora apiculata Bl.	R
Rhizophora mucronata Poir	R
Rubiaceae	
Borreria alata (Aubl.) DC.	A
Borreria articularis (L. f.) F. N. Will.	C
Borreria laevicaulis (Miq.) Ridl.	C
Borreria setidens (Miq.) Bold.	C
Diodia acymifolia (Willd. ex. Roem. & Schult.) Bremek.	A
Guettarda speciosa L.	R
Hedyotis corymbosa (L.) Lamk.	C
Ixora congesta Roxb.	R
Morinda citrifolia L.	A
Morinda umbellata L.	C
Oxyceros longiflora (Lamk.) Yamazaki	R
Scyphiphora hydrophyllacea Gaertn. f.	R
Tarenna costata (Miq.) Merr..	R
Tarenna fragrans (Nees) K. & V.	R
Timonius compressicaulis (Miq.) Boerl.	N
Timonius wallichinus (Korth.) Valeton	R
Rutaceae	
Melicope lunu-ankenda (Gaertn.) T. G.Hartley	R
Murraya koenigii (L.) Spreng.	S
Santalaceae	
Dendrotrophe varians (Bl.) Miq.	R

Sapindaceae	
Allophyllus cobbe (L.) Racusch.	R
Guioa pleuropteris (Bl.) Radlk.	R
Mischocarpus sundaicus Bl.	R
Nephelium lappaceum L.	S
Sapotaceae	
Planchonella obovata (R. Br.) Pierre	R
Scrophulariaceae	
Limnophila sessiliflora Bl.	R
Lindernia antipoda (L.) Alston	R
Lindernia crustacea (L.) F.v. M.	C
Lindernia sessiliflora (Benth.) Wettst.	R
Scoparia dulcis L.	A
Simaroubaceae	
Brucea javanica (L.) Merr.	R
Eurycoma longifolia Jack	R
Smilacaceae	
Smilax megacarpa DC.	R
Solanaceae	
Physalis minima L.	C
Solanum melongena L.	S
Solanum torvum Sw.	A
Sonneratiaceae	
Sonneratia alba J. J. Smith	C
Sonneratia ovata Backer	N
Sterculiaceae	
Commersonia bartramia (L.) Merr.	C
Heritiera littoralis Dryand. ex W. Ait.	R
Pterospermum diversifolium Bl.	R
Symplocaceae	
Symplocos fasciculata Zoll.	R
Theaceae	
Adinandra dumosa Jack	C
Eurya acuminata DC.	C

Thymclaceae	
Linostoma pauciflorum Griff.	R
Tiliaceae	
Brownlowia tersa (L.) Kosterm	N
Triumfetta rhomboidea Jacq.	R
Turncraceae	
Turnera ulmifolia L.	A
Typhaceae	
Typha angustifolia L.	A
Ulmaceae	
Trema cannabina Lour.	C
Trema tomentosa (Roxb.) Hara	C
Umbelliferae	
Centella asiatica (L.) Urb.	C
Urticaceae	
Laportea interrupta (L.) Chew	C
Verbenaceae	
Clerodendrum inerme (L.) Gaertn.	R
Clerodendrum laevifolium Bl.	R
Clerodendrum paniculatum L.	S
Clerodendrum philippinum Schauer	S
Clerodendrum villosum Bl.	R
Gmelina asiatica L.	C
Lantana camara L.	A
Premna corymbosa (Burm. f.) Rottl. & Willd.	R
Stachytarpheta indica (L.) Vahl	C
Vitex pinnata L.	C
Vitex trifolia L.	R
Vitaceae	
Ampelocissus elegans (Kurz.) Gegnep.	R
Cissus hastata (Miq) Planch.	C
Zingiberaceae	
Languas galanga (L.) Stuntz.	S

The Mammals of Pulau Ubin — A Checklist

C = Common, U = Uncommon, S = Scarce, R = Resident,
F = Feral, V = Visitor

	Common Name	Scientific Name	
1	Sunda Pangolin	*Manis javanica*	SR
2	House Shrew	*Suncus murinus*	CR
3	Large Flying Fox	*Pteropus vampyrus*	UV
4	Lesser Dog-faced Fruit Bat	*Cynopterus brachyotis*	CR
5	Long-tongued Nectar Bat	*Macroglossus minimus*	SR
6	Pouched Tomb Bat	*Taphozous saccolaimus*	CR
7	Whiskered Myotis	*Myotis muricola*	CR
8	Grey Large-footed Myotis	*Myotis adversus*	CR
9	Lesser Asiatic Yellow House Bat	*Scotophilus kuhlii*	CR
10	Greater Bamboo Bat	*Tylonycteris robustula*	CR
11	Long-tailed Macaque	*Macaca fascicularis*	CR
12	Oriental Small-clawed Otter	*Aonyx cinerea*	SR
13	Common Palm Civet	*Paradoxurus hermaphroditus*	UR
14	Leopard Cat	*Prionailurus bengalensis*	SR
15	Indo-Pacific Humpback Dolphin	*Sousa chinensis*	SR
16	Dugong	*Dugong dugon*	SR
17	Asian Elephant	*Elephas maximus*	SV
18	Malayan Tapir	*Tapirus indicus*	SV
19	Wild Pig	*Sus scrofa*	UR
20	Plantain Squirrel	*Callosciurus notatus*	CR
21	House Mouse	*Mus musculus*	CR
22	House Rat	*Rattus rattus*	CR
23	Malaysian Wood Rat	*Rattus tiomanicus*	UR
24	Annandale's Rat	*Rattus annandalei*	CR
25	Polynesian Rat	*Rattus exulans*	CR

The Birds of Pulau Ubin — A Checklist

Latin names and most common names used follow "An Annotated Checklist of the Birds of the Oriental Region" by Tim Inskipp, Nigel Lindsey & William Duckworth (1996). The checklist order mainly remains faithful to Peter's sequence for easy reference to the best existing field guides of this region.

C = Common, U = Uncommon, S = Scarce
R = Resident, M = Migrant, V = Visitor, I = Introduction

#	Common name	Latin name	Status
1	Swinhoe's Storm-petrel	*Oceandromus monorhis*	SM
2	Christmas Frigatebird	*Fregata andrewsi*	SV
3	Great-billed Heron	*Ardea sumatrana*	SV
4	Grey Heron	*Ardea cinerea*	UV
5	Purple Heron	*Ardea purpurea*	UV
6	Striated Heron	*Butorides striatus*	CR
7	Little Egret	*Egretta garzetta*	CM
8	Pacific Reef-Egret	*Egretta sacra*	CR
9	Chinese Egret	*Egretta eulophotes*	SM
10	Great Egret	*Casmerodius alba*	UM
11	Cattle Egret	*Bubulcus ibis*	SM
12	Black-crowned Night Heron	*Nycticorax nycticorax*	UV
13	Yellow Bittern	*Ixobrychus sinensis*	UM
14	Schrenck's Bittern	*Ixobrychus eurhythmus*	SM
15	Cinnamon Bittern	*Ixobrychus cinnamomeus*	UM
16	Osprey	*Pandion haliaetus*	UM
17	Black Baza	*Aviceda leuphotes*	CM
18	Oriental Honey-Buzzard	*Pernis ptilorhyncus*	CM
19	Black-winged Kite	*Elanus caeruleus*	UV
20	Brahminy Kite	*Haliastur indus*	CR
21	White-bellied Fish-Eagle	*Haliaeetus leucogaster*	CR
22	Crested Serpent-Eagle	*Spilornis cheela*	SV
23	Japanese Sparrowhawk	*Accipiter gularis*	CM
24	Crested Goshawk	*Accipiter trivirgatus*	SV
25	Chinese Goshawk	*Accipiter soloensis*	UM
26	Grey-faced Buzzard	*Butastur indicus*	SM
27	Common Buzzard	*Buteo buteo*	SM
28	Changeable Hawk-Eagle	*Spizaetus cirrhatus*	SR
29	Eurasian Hobby	*Falco subbuteo*	SM
30	Peregrine Falcon	*Falco peregrinus*	SM
31	Blue-breasted Quail	*Coturnix chinensis*	SV
32	Red Junglefowl	*Gallus gallus*	CR
33	Barred Buttonquail	*Turnix suscitator*	UR
34	Red-legged Crake	*Rallina fasciata*	SR
35	White-breasted Waterhen	*Amaurornis phoenicurus*	CR
36	Watercock	*Gallicrex cinerea*	SM
37	Grey Plover	*Pluvialis squatarola*	UM
38	Pacific Golden Plover	*Pluvialis fulva*	CM
39	Little Ringed Plover	*Charadrius dubius*	UM
40	Lesser Sand-plover	*Charadrius mongolus*	CM
41	Greater Sand-plover	*Charadrius leschenaultii*	UM
42	Eurasian Curlew	*Numenius arquata*	UM
43	Whimbrel	*Numenius phaeopus*	CM
44	Bar-tailed Godwit	*Limosa lapponica*	UM
45	Common Redshank	*Tringa totanus*	CM
46	Marsh Sandpiper	*Tringa stagnatillis*	CM
47	Common Greenshank	*Tringa nebularia*	CM
48	Wood Sandpiper	*Tringa glareola*	UM
49	Terek Sandpiper	*Xenus cinereus*	UM
50	Common Sandpiper	*Actitis hypoleucos*	CM
51	Ruddy Turnstone	*Arenaria interpres*	UM
52	Asian Dowitcher	*Limnodromas semipalmatus*	UM
53	Pintail Snipe	*Gallinago stenura*	UM
54	Red-necked Stint	*Calidris ruficollis*	UM
55	Curlew Sandpiper	*Calidris ferruginea*	CM
56	Broad-billed Sandpiper	*Limicola falcinellus*	SM
57	Black-headed Gull	*Larus ridibundus*	UM
58	White-winged Tern	*Chlidonias leucopterus*	CM
59	Gull-billed Tern	*Gelochelidon nilotica*	UM
60	Common Tern	*Sterna hirundo*	UM
61	Black-naped Tern	*Sterna sumatrana*	UR
62	Bridled Tern	*Sterna anaethetus*	SM
63	Little Tern	*Sterna albifrons*	CM
64	Great Crested Tern	*Sterna bergii*	CM
65	Lesser Crested Tern	*Sterna bengalensis*	UM
66	Cinnamon-headed Green Pigeon	*Treron fulvicollis*	UV
67	Little Green-Pigeon	*Treron olax*	UV
68	Pink-necked Green-Pigeon	*Treron vernans*	CR
69	Jambu Fruit-dove	*Ptilinopus jambu*	UV
70	Green Imperial Pigeon	*Ducula aenea*	SV
71	Rock Pigeon	*Columba livia*	CI
72	Red Collared-dove	*Streptopelia tranquebarica*	UI
73	Spotted Dove	*Streptopelia chinensis*	CR
74	Zebra Dove	*Geopelia striata*	CR
75	Emerald Dove	*Chalcophaps indica*	UR
76	Rose-ringed Parakeet	*Psittacula krameri*	UI
77	Red-breasted Parakeet	*Psittacula alexandri*	UI
78	Long-tailed Parakeet	*Psittacula longicauda*	CR
79	Blue-crowned Hanging Parrot	*Loriculus galgulus*	SV
80	Chestnut-winged Cuckoo	*Clamator coromandus*	UM
81	Indian Cuckoo	*Cuculus micropterus*	CM
82	Plaintive Cuckoo	*Cacomantis merulinus*	SR
83	Rusty-breasted cuckoo	*Cacomantis sepulcralis*	UR
84	Little Bronze-Cuckoo	*Chrysococcyx minutillus*	UR
85	Drongo Cuckoo	*Surniculus lugubris*	UM
86	Asian Koel	*Eudynamys scolopacea*	CR
87	Chestnut-bellied Malkoha	*Phaenicophaeus sumatranus*	SV
88	Greater Coucal	*Centropus sinensis*	UR
89	Lesser Coucal	*Centropus bengalensis*	UR
90	Barn Owl	*Tyto alba*	SR
91	Collared Scops-Owl	*Otus bakkamoena*	CR
92	Buffy Fish Owl	*Ketupa ketupu*	SR
93	Brown Hawk-Owl	*Ninox scutulata*	UV
94	Spotted Wood-Owl	*Strix seloputo*	SR
95	Large-tailed Nightjar	*Caprimulgus macrurus*	CR
96	Savanna Nightjar	*Caprimulgus affinis*	SR
97	Edible-nest Swiftlet	*Callocalia fuciphage*	CR
98	Himalayan Swiftlet	*Callocalia brevirostris*	UM
99	Fork-tailed Swift	*Apus pacificus*	CM
100	House Swift	*Apus affinis*	CR
101	Asia Palm Swift	*Cypsiurus balasiensis*	UR
102	Common Kingfisher	*Alcedo atthis*	CM
103	Stork-billed Kingfisher	*Halcyon capensis*	UR
104	Ruddy Kingfisher	*Halcyon coromanda*	SM
105	White-throated Kingfisher	*Halcyon smyrnensis*	CR
106	Black-capped Kingfisher	*Halcyon pileata*	UM
107	Collared Kingfisher	*Todiramphus chloris*	CR
108	Blue-tailed Bee-eater	*Merops phillippinus*	CM
109	Blue-throated Bee-eater	*Merops viridis*	CR
110	Dollarbird	*Eurystomus orientalis*	UR/CM
111	Oriental Pied Hornbill	*Anthracoceros albirostris*	SR/SV
112	Rufous Woodpecker	*Celeus brachyurus*	SR
113	Laced Woodpecker	*Picus vittatus*	CR
114	Banded Woodpecker	*Picus miniaceus*	SV
115	Common Flameback	*Dinopium javanense*	CR
116	Sunda Pygmy Woodpecker	*Dendrocopus moluccensis*	UR
117	Blue-winged Pitta	*Pitta moluccensis*	SM
118	Mangrove Pitta	*Pitta megarhyncha*	SR
119	Barn Swallow	*Hirundo rustica*	CM
120	Pacific Swallow	*Hirundo tahitica*	CR
121	Red-rumped Swallow	*Hirundo daurica*	CM
122	Pied Triller	*Lalage nigra*	UR
123	Ashy Minivet	*Pericrocotus divaricatus*	UM
124	Common Iora	*Aegithina tiphia*	CR
125	Straw-headed Bulbul	*Pycnonotus zeylanicus*	CR
126	Black-headed Bulbul	*Pycnonotus atriceps*	SV
127	Red-whiskered Bulbul	*Pyconotus jocosus*	SI
128	Yellow-vented Bulbul	*Pycnonotus goiavier*	CR
129	Olive-winged Bulbul	*Pycnonotus plumosus*	CR
130	Ashy Bulbul	*Hemixos flavala*	UV
131	Crow-billed Drongo	*Dicrurus annectans*	UM
132	Black-naped Oriole	*Oriolus chinensis*	CR
133	House Crow	*Corvus splendens*	CI
134	Large-billed Crow	*Corvus macrorhynchos*	CR
135	White-chested Babbler	*Trichastoma rostratum*	SR
136	Abbott's Babbler	*Malacocincla abbotti*	UR
137	Siberian Blue Robin	*Luscinia cyane*	UM
138	Oriental Magpie Robi	*Copsychus saularis*	CR
139	White-rumped Shama	*Copsychus malabaricus*	UR
140	Golden-bellied Gerygone	*Gerygone sulphurea*	CR
141	Arctic Warbler	*Phylloscopus borealis*	CM
142	Easter Crowned Warbler	*Phylloscopus coronatus*	SM
143	Oriental Reed Warbler	*Acrocephalus orientalis*	UM
144	Black-browed Reed Warbler	*Acrocephalus bistrigiceps*	SM
145	Common Tailorbird	*Orthotomus sutorius*	CR
146	Dark-necked Tailorbird	*Orthotomus atrogularis*	CR
147	Ashy Tailorbird	*Orthotomus ruficeps*	CR
148	Rufous-tailed Tailorbird	*Orthotomus sericeus*	CR
149	Yellow-bellied Prinia	*Prinia flaviventris*	UR
150	Asian Brown Flycatcher	*Muscicapa dauurica*	CM
151	Yellow-rumped Flycatcher	*Ficedula zanthopygia*	UM
152	Mangrove Blue Flycatcher	*Cyornis rufigastra*	SV
153	Pied Fantail	*Rhipidura javanica*	CR
154	Black-naped Monarch	*Hypothymis azurea*	SV
155	Asian Paradise-Flycatcher	*Terpsiphone paradisi*	UM
156	Mangrove Whistler	*Pachycephala grisola*	SR
157	Yellow Wagtail	*Motacilla flava*	UM
158	Forest Wagtail	*Dendronanthus indicus*	UM
159	Brown Shrike	*Lanius cristatus*	UM
160	Tiger Shrike	*Lanius tigrinus*	UM
161	Asian Glossy Starling	*Aplonis panayensis*	CR
162	Purple-backed Starling	*Stumus sturninus*	UM
163	Common Myna	*Acridotheres tristis*	CR
164	Javan Myna	*Acridotheres javanicus*	CI
165	Hill Myna	*Gracula religiosa*	UR
166	Brown-throated Sunbird	*Anthreptes malacensis*	CR
167	Purple-throated Sunbird	*Nectarinia sperata*	CR
168	Copper-throated Sunbird	*Nectarinia calcostetha*	CR
169	Olive-backed Sunbird	*Nectarinia jugularis*	CR
170	Crimson Sunbird	*Aethopyga siparaja*	CR
171	Yellow-eared Spiderhunter	*Arachnothera chrysogenys*	SV
172	Orange–bellied Flowerpecker	*Dicaeum trigonostigma*	SR
173	Scarlet-backed Flowerpecker	*Dicaeum cruentatum*	CR
174	Eurasian Tree Sparrow	*Passer montanus*	CR
175	White-rumped Munia	*Lonchura striata*	SR
176	Javan Munia	*Lonchura leucogastroides*	SI
177	Scaly-breasted Munia	*Lonchura punctulata*	CR
178	Black-headed Munia	*Lonchura malacca*	CR
179	White-headed Munia	*Lonchura maja*	SR

References

Briffett, Clive and Ho Hua Chew, eds. *State of the Natural Environment in Singapore.* Singapore: Nature Society (S), June 1999.

Burris, Samuel J. "The White Girl of Pulau Ubin." *Changi*, Nov 1993.

Chua Ee Kiam. *Nature in Singapore — Ours to Protect.* Singapore: Nature Society (S), 1993.

Conservation Proposal for Pulau Ubin. Singapore: Nature Society (S) Conservation Committee, Feb 1992.

Hails, Christopher and Frank Jarvis. *Birds of Singapore.* Singapore: Times Editions, 1988.

Hall-Jones, John. *The Thomson Paintings — Mid-Nineteenth Century Paintings of the Straits Settlements and Malaya.* Singapore: Oxford University Press, 1983.

Huang Yi Jun et al, Prof Edmund Waller, ed. "Pulau Ubin — Sustaining the Rural Episodes." NUS School of Architecture, Level II 98/99, National University of Singapore.

Khoo Khay Choong et al. *Crop Pests and their Management in Malaysia.* Kuala Lumpur: Tropical Press Sdn Bhd, 1991.

Lim, Francis and Monty Lee. *Fascinating Snakes of Southeast Asia.* Kuala Lumpur: Tropical Press Sdn Bhd, 1989.

Lim, Kelvin and Francis Lim. *A Guide to Amphibians and Reptiles of Singapore.* Singapore: Singapore Science Centre, 1992.

Low, Edna. "Pulau Ubin — the Exodus." Department of Sociology, National University of Singapore, 1995.

Low Foo Yong, Ooi Hui Mei and Han Gee Nam. *The OBS Story.* Singapore: People's Association, 1997.

MacKinnon, John and Karen Phillips. *A Field Guide to the Birds of Borneo, Sumatra, Java and Bali.* New York: Oxford University Press, 1993.

Neo Say Hian, Steven. *A Guide to Common Butterflies of Singapore.* Singapore: Singapore Science Centre, 1996.

Ng, Peter and N. Sivasothi, eds. *A Guide to the Mangroves of Singapore I and II.* Singapore: Singapore Science Centre, 1999.

Ong Hoon Siang, ed. "Pulau Ubin — Ecology and Site Planning Elective: Landscape Architecture." Year 4 NUS 1990/91 Students, School of Architecture, National University of Singapore.

"Pulau Ubin — Nature in a Balance." *Nature Watch*, Vol 3, No 3, 1995.

Quek-Anne Hong Eng. "The Chinese Family in Pulau Ubin." Department of Sociology, National University of Singapore, 1977.

Recollections — Peoples and Places. Singapore: Oral History Department, 1990.

Strange, Morten and Allen Jeyarajasingam. *Birds — A Photographic Guide to the Birds of Peninsular Malaysia and Singapore.* Singapore: Sun Tree Publishing, 1993.

Tan, Hugh T. W., K. S. Chua, B. C. Soong, I. M. Turner and Ali Ibrahim. "Plant Life" (unpublished data).

The Japanese Occupation 1942-1945: A Pictorial Record of Singapore during the War. Singapore: Times Editions for National Archives of Singapore, 1966.

Turner, I. M., Hugh T. W. Tan, K. S. Chua, Haji Samsuri bin Haji Ahmad and Y. C. Wee. "A Botanical Survey of Pulau Ubin." *The Gardens Bulletin*, Singapore Vol 44 (Part 1) June 1992.

Index

Acknowledgements

A great many institutions and individuals have helped in one way or another in the making of this book. I wish to thank:

- Dr Tan Wee Kiat, CEO National Parks Board, for his support, and his staff members for facilitating my movements around the island, gaining access to the granite quarries and for permission to use the aerial photographs.
- COL Winston Lim (Outward Bound Singapore) for permission to photograph the activities of OBS, and the support of his staff, especially Jeremy Tay, Teo Beng Tiam, Gregory Baptist and Terence Lee.
- Commandant NPCC, Mr Yong Khin Chong, and Seong Then Yee (National Police Cadet Corps) for his help in the photography of NPCC activities.
- Members of the Nature Society, Singapore (NSS), for introducing to me a fecund world of diverse flora and fauna that has gone largely unnoticed. The night surveys by the Vertebrate Group are a highlight of my memories of the island.
- Mr Lim Chye Joo, for permission to use the class photo of the Bin Kiang School and for all the wonderful stories about the island.
- Mr Pang Teng Khoon, for permission to use his painting (p. 59).
- Dr John Hall-Jones, the great grandson of John Turnbull Thomson, for permission to use two images (Pulo Ubin Granite Quarries, 1851 and Grooved stones on Pulo Ubin near Singapore, 1850) from *The Thomson Paintings: Mid-Nineteenth Century Paintings of the Straits Settlements and Malaya.*
- Professor David Orr, for permission to use excerpts of his speech.
- The National Archives of Singapore, Ministry of Information and the Arts and The Straits Times for permission to use images from their collection.
- Robert Teo (for his invaluable help), Ali Ibrahim (flora), Tham Fong Yee (fungi), Dr Francis Seow-Choen (stick insect).
- Richard Lim and Mrs Tan Phaik Yin (Ministry of Health — for their input on the M&CH clinic).
- Professor Edmund Waller & his students at the School of Architecture especially Huang Yijun.
- Chee Gin San, former owner of Aik Hwa Granite Quarry, for information on the quarrying works.
- Sutari bin Supari, for helping to conduct some of the interviews with residents.
- Subaraj Rajathurai, for his input and list of mammals and birds.
- Billy Kon, Tan Siok Hwee, Loh Jing Ling, Jeremy Chua, Andy Ho and Tony Lim — they were all wonderful companions.
- Miss Wong Siow Kian for the exclusive tapir shot (p. 32, right) and together with her sister Sook Kuan offered us what we fondly remember as the trademark "Ubin hospitality".
- William Tan and his sons, Herbert and Bernard, who showed us the bomb shelters and a photograph of a pangolin they found on the island (p. 111, bottom).
- Mr Ong Leong Choon, Manager of the Ubin Community Centre, for the press reports on Ubin.
- Dr Audrey Ng who helped to translate the Chinese newspapers.
- Mr Lee Watt Sim for his sharing his recollections.
- The assistance from Wang Luan Keng and Bryan Wong is not forgotten.
- The many residents of Pulau Ubin who did not mind the intrusion into their world and for sharing with us their stories.
- And the generous donors — the "Friends of Ubin" who cared enough to want to see the beauty of Ubin in print.

PHOTOGRAPHERS

The many photographers who struggled to document the many faces of Pulau Ubin deserve more than praise. Lugging the heavy photographic equipment around the whole island reflects the passions and dedication of these people concerned with the fragile wilderness. And the many occasions they had to venture in, under unpredictable weather and often not a wonderful slide to show the amount of effort. But they still persevered. I take my hat off to them.

PHOTO CREDITS

All photographs in this book are by Chua Ee Kiam except for the following:

National Archives of Singapore: 33 (right), 34 (bottom left), 37 (left, Collection of Quek Tiong Swee), 37 (right and top right)
Outward Bound Singapore: 120 (right)
The Straits Times: 85, 110 (bottom)

Ali Ibrahim: front cover (right), 10 (right), 22-23, 46 (bottom left), 58 (top), 62 (right), 80 (left), 92 (bottom left), 93 (bottom and right), 111 (centre), 116, 139
Jimmy Chew: 28-29, 45, 55 (top inset), 87, 101 (centre), 124 (top), 129

Elfie Eleza Kamarudin: 109 (bottom left)
Andy Ho: front cover (left), 11 (bottom right), 60, 71 (top), 83, 95 (right inset), 112, 125
Dr John Hall-Jones: 27 (top), 32 (left)
Billy Kon: 17 (right), 25 (left), 35, 38 (left), 46 (bottom right), 54 (left), 65, 73, 72 (top), 109 (top), 121 (top right and bottom), 122, 123 (left)
Lee King Lee: 86, 106 (top left), 115 (top), 126, back cover (inset)
Tony Lim: 31 (top right and bottom)
Ong Kiem Sian: 89 (bottom right), 94 (top left), 96 (bottom inset), 97 (top and bottom left), 99 (bottom), 114, 121 (top left)
Phang Tuck Pew: 95 (left), 96 (top left inset), 98 (bottom), 102 (bottom left), 103 (top left), 104 (top centre)
Raymond Poon: 16 (top and bottom right), 94 (top right and bottom)
Jacky Soh: 108 (left), 110 (top), 118 (top)
Mohamad Yusoff: 62 (left).
Morten Strange: 6, 12, 123 (right)
Robert Teo: 101 (top right), 103 (top right), 106 (bottom right), 107 (left), 108 (right)
Sutari bin Supari: 15
Wong Tuan Wah: cover backdrop, endpapers, 24, 33 (left), 88, 140.

Friends of Ubin

This book was made possible through the generous support of the following:

Marine Parade Community Development Council (CDC)

National Parks Board (NParks)

Sponsors

Kodak (Singapore) Pte Ltd
William Toh (Cathay Photo Pte Ltd)
Kay Hian Pte Ltd

Francis Ng, Helen Chee & Judy Ng
Dr Eu Oy Chu, Yeo Khee Chye & Yeo Ying Hao
Dr Lim Sor Kheng, Quek Chin Heng & Linus Ong
Dr Michael Leong, Irene Ong, Annabel Leong & Aaron Leong
Tan Dib Jin, Gary G. Tan & Daryl Raizal-Ming Tan
Toh Sew Lay